THE
SEEN
AND THE
UNSEEN

JERRY CROSSLEY

The Seen and the Unseen
Copyright © 2019 **Jerry Crossley**

All rights reserved. No part of this book may be used or reproduced by any means, graphic, electronic, or mechanical, including photocopying, recording, taping or by information storage and retrieval system without the written permission of the author except in the case of brief quotations embodied in critical articles and reviews.

Stratton Press Publishing
831 N Tatnall Street Suite M #188,
Wilmington, DE 19801
www.stratton-press.com
1-888-323-7009

Because of the dynamic nature of the Internet, any web addresses or links contained in this book may have changed since publication and may no longer be valid. The views expressed in the work are solely those of the author and do not necessarily reflect the views of the publisher, and the publisher hereby disclaims any responsibility for them.

Any people depicted in stock imagery provided by Shutterstock are models, and such images are being used for illustrative purposes only.

ISBN (Paperback): 978-1-64345-026-1
ISBN (Paperback): 978-1-64345-387-3
ISBN (Ebook): 978-1-64345-212-8

Printed in the United States of America

So we fix our eyes not on what is seen, but on what is unseen. For what is seen is temporary, but what is unseen is eternal.

—2 Corinthians 4:18

Truly you are a God who hides Himself, O God and Savior of Israel.

—Isaiah 45:15

Now to the King eternal, immortal, invisible, the only God, be honor and glory for ever and ever. Amen.

—1 Timothy 1:17

Immortal, invisible, God only wise,
In light inaccessible hid from our eyes.
Most blessed, most glorious, the Ancient of Days,
Almighty, victorious—Thy great name we praise!

Great Father of glory, pure Father of light,
Thine angels adore Thee, all veiling their sight;
All praise we would render: O help us to see
Tis only the splendor of light hideth thee!

—Walter Chalmers Smith,
"Immortal, Invisible" (1876)

> By faith [Moses] left Egypt, not fearing the king's anger; he persevered because he saw him who is invisible.
>
> —Hebrews 11:27

> By faith we understand that the universe was formed at God's command, so that what is seen was not made out of what was visible.
>
> —Hebrews 11:3

> We live by faith, not by sight.
>
> —2 Corinthians 5:7

> I ask no dream, no prophet ecstasies,
> No sudden rending of the veil of clay,
> No angel visitant, no opening skies;
> But take the dimness of my soul away.
>
> —George Croly, "Spirit of God, Descend Upon My Heart" (1854)

Therefore we do not lose heart. Though outwardly we are wasting away, yet inwardly we are being renewed day by day. For our light and momentary troubles are achieving for us an eternal glory that far outweighs them all. So we fix our eyes not on what is seen, but on what is unseen. For what is seen is temporary, but what is unseen is eternal.

—2 Corinthians 4:16–18

Now faith is being sure of what we hope for and certain of what we do not see.

—Hebrews 11:1

And, Lord, haste the day when my faith shall be sight,
The clouds be rolled back as a scroll…

—Horatio G. Spafford, "It Is Well With My Soul" (1873)

You will seek me and find me when you seek me with all your heart. I will be found by you.

—Jeremiah 29:13–14a

Now we see but a poor reflection as in a mirror; then we shall see face to face.

—1 Corinthians 13:12a

He is a God who works "behind the scenes;" he is also a God who, unseen, works behind the "seens."

—Jerry Crossley

Faith is believing what you do not see, and the reward of faith is seeing what you believe.

—Huston Smith (*Guideposts*; 39 Seminary Hill Rd., Carmel, NY 10512; Aug. 2002; "Why Faith Matters Today;" pp. 33–35)

One sees clearly only with the heart; what is essential is invisible to the eye.

—Antoine de Saint-Exupéry, *The Little Prince* (1900–1944)

Unless otherwise noted, Scripture quotations are taken from the HOLY BIBLE, NEW INTERNATIONAL VERSION, Copyright @ 1973, 1978, 1984 by International Bible Society. Used by permission of Zondervan Publishing House.

Scripture references marked KJV are from the King James Version of the Bible.

CONTENTS

Foreword 11

Acknowledgments 13

Chapter 1: The Seen and the Unseen..........................15

Chapter 2: The Hidden and Revealed.........................20

Chapter 3: "Truth" Turned Upside Down 24

Chapter 4: Taken By Surprise! 29

Chapter 5: Three Great Wishes...................................33

Chapter 6: Fear of the Future 38

Chapter 7: Doubt and Trust.......................................43

Chapter 8: His Everlasting Arms 48

Chapter 9: Perseverance..52

Chapter 10: Disappointment with Others..................57

Chapter 11: "Disappointment with God" 62

Chapter 12: Faith In Spite Of..68

Chapter 13: Guilt..72

Chapter 14: Trials...77

Chapter 15: The Need to Forgive 81

Chapter 16: Praise!...85

Chapter 17: "Nevertheless…" 90

Chapter 18: Failure 94

Chapter 19: Interruptions: Time Out for God 99

Chapter 20: Joy..104

Chapter 21: Worry...108

Chapter 22: Rejection 113

Chapter 23: The Shattered Dream.......................................117

Chapter 24: Suffering..122

Chapter 25: Hopelessness...126

Chapter 26: "It Is Well with My Soul".................................131

Chapter 27: Listening Prayer..135

Chapter 28: The Twenty-Third Psalm.................................139

Chapter 29: "The Silence of God" 145

Chapter 30: "At Every Corner"...149

A Closing Prayer 155

Endnotes..157

FOREWORD

Sometimes life can be upsettingly capricious, sending unanticipated circumstances our way, dumping them unceremoniously upon our doorstep, and obligating us to deal with them. There are times—just when everything seems to be going well—that the rug suddenly is yanked from under our feet and we are sent sprawling. In those discomfiting, bewildering moments, we desperately search for firm ground on which to stand.

For half a century I have pastored churches in the mountains, in towns, in the city, and finally, in a small village. In spite of my longevity, I cannot legitimately advance the claim that "I have seen it all," but I have seen a lot, heard a lot, and learned a lot about human nature and the nature of God.

Our language is inadequate to describe the things of God. In his book, *The Bible Speaks To You*,[1] Robert McAfee Brown explained that in utilizing language to describe eternal dimensions, we are attempting to describe that which is beyond the limits of our human expression and experience. He noted that it is like the task of an artist who is portraying railroad tracks in his painting. He paints their convergence on the horizon. Of course, they do not ever really meet but continue to run parallel. Yet this is the best he can do in his effort to describe a three-dimensional world in terms of a two-dimensional canvas. In a similar way, we resort to the language of metaphor in our attempt to describe a multidimensional God in terms our three-dimensional world. It will necessarily result in distortion, being true and not true simultaneously.

We have to look more deeply. St. Paul wrote, "Therefore we do not lose heart. Though outwardly we are wasting away, yet inwardly we are being renewed day by day. For our light and momentary troubles are achieving for us an eternal glory that far outweighs them all. So we fix our eyes not on what is seen, but on what is unseen. For what is seen is temporary, but what is unseen is eternal" (2 Cor. 4:16–18)—the "seen and the unseen!" We tend to respond to what we *can* see: the problems that surround and beset us. What we tend to miss are all those things we *cannot* see: the promises, presence, and providence of God. This book is about these unseen things.

It is my sincere hope, that along the way, you will discover some passage that illuminates your path ahead. Furthermore, it is my prayer that, on your own spiritual journey, you will develop a "third eye," an inner vision that is able to see the unseen fingerprints of God.

ACKNOWLEDGMENTS

My book seems to be a compendium of wisdom that others along the way have shared with me. I would like to acknowledge my debt to the following:

1. Kathy and Bob Dillon (chapter 3), who gave me a motorcycle, along with their blessings, which I needed as I learned to drive it. The motorcycle taught me countless spiritual lessons and brought me closer to God than I intended.
2. Judy Donnelly (chapter 3), who shared with me her deeply spiritual insight into Matthew 6:19–21.
3. Joyce Dence (chapter 4), for her profound understanding of the way God sometimes works. She truly saw, with a "third eye," the Unseen.
4. Bob and Sandy Allesandrini (chapter 11), who courageously shared with me their faithful response to a most terrible moment in their life.
5. Ron Susek (chapter 11), for his insight into suffering and the caring and creative way God uses it to shape us into the image of His Son.
6. Reverend Carl Swansen (chapter 14), Director of Development at Lankenau Hospital, for his discernment

regarding how to pray for someone between life and death. His deep wisdom freed me from the anxiety that I might be praying at cross-purposes with God and helped me to see God's presence in the life of another.
7. Lee Zengeler (chapter 16), for her insight into worship and praise. First comes the act of praise, and then comes the feeling of joy. It is not the other way around.
8. Dr. Richard Leaver (chapter 19). His brazen prayer of self-surrender would teach me something about the providence of God.
9. Jean Gabl (chapter 22), our own daughter, who shared her faith without embarrassment and ministered to a little student who was desperately in need.
10. My typist, Janet Neill, who graciously offered me her secretarial skills and, as a result, made my manuscript clearer and smoother.

For each of these great people of God, I give God thanks.

Chapter 1

THE SEEN AND THE UNSEEN

The Introductory Message

Long ago, in the course of my pastoral ministry, which has lasted half a century, I discovered a passage of Scripture that stirred my heart and stimulated my imagination: 2 Corinthians 4:16–18. There the apostle Paul spoke about "the seen and the unseen." He wrote, "So we fix our eyes not on what is seen, but on what is unseen. For what is seen is temporary, but what is unseen is eternal."

It seems to me that most people, including Christians, tend to focus on all the problems they see around them. They soon feel overwhelmed and begin to entertain the thought of giving up. They think that maybe they will just go back to bed and pull the covers over their heads. They respond to what they can see: all the troubles that spread in front of them like a minefield.

What people forget is precisely what they cannot see: *the invisible presence of God!* In Hebrews, it says, "Now faith is being…certain of what we do not see" (Heb. 11:1). And what is that again? The invisible presence of God! In 1 Timothy we read, "Now to the King eternal, immortal, *invisible*, the only God, be honor and glory forever and ever. Amen" (1 Tim. 1:17; emphasis mine). In Hebrews we read, "By faith [Moses] left Egypt, not fearing the king's anger; he persevered because he saw him who is *invisible*" (Heb. 11:27; emphasis mine).

So it is that I present the first and foundational message in a series that focuses on victorious Christian living: our problems, his presence. Far back in Isaiah, these words were inscribed, "He gives strength to the weary and increases the power of the weak. Even youths grow tired and weary, and young men stumble and fall; but those who hope in the Lord will renew their strength. They will soar on wings like eagles; they will run and not grow weary, they will walk and not be faint" (Isa. 40:29–31).

In the year 1972, I was the pastor of a little church in the town of Croydon, Bucks County, Pennsylvania. Croydon was predominately a blue-collar, working class community that was located at the junction of Neshaminy Creek and the Delaware River. At that time, even though I had been a pastor for more than a decade, I was making only the minimum salary, and I was married with two children. Then our sister-in-law, at age thirty-two, lost her battle with cancer, and we took her two children to raise. We now had two ten-year-old boys and two eight-year-old girls to provide for on a very small salary. Furthermore, this congregation had previously had three wonderful pastors, and I was not one of them! To say that I felt inadequate as a provider is an understatement. I could not have been more discouraged. I was done. I felt like quitting and began to doubt that I ever had been called by God in the first place!

There's an old story—probably apocryphal—that resurfaces over the years. It is the story of a farmer who, taking a break from drudgery, one day glanced into the sky and saw the letters *PC* forming in the clouds. He puzzled over what this must mean and concluded that the vision was instructing him to "Preach Christ!"

Yes, he thought, PC *means "preach Christ."*

So the farmer sold his farm and became a preacher. He was terrible at his job. Someone in fact questioned his "calling," listened to his explanation of the mystical letters in the sky, and then gingerly asked, "Did you ever stop to consider that the letters *PC* might simply have meant 'plant corn'?"

I was starting to feel like that poor farmer. Maybe I should be planting corn and had gotten my signals mixed up. Late one night, after my wife had gone to bed, I started talking to the Lord. "Oh God," I stammered, "I am such an earthen vessel. I am just clay, just dirt!"

Suddenly a complete thought telepathically popped into my head. I knew it was the Lord's response: *"But you have this treasure that I have given you. Stop focusing your eyes on yourself, and start fixing your eyes on the treasure!"*

I then recalled the verse in 2 Corinthians that says, "But we have this treasure in jars of clay to show that this all-surpassing power is from God and not from us" (2 Cor. 4:7). In other words, I was hearing the Lord telling me to stop looking at the seen and to look instead at the unseen.

A Roman Catholic priest whose name was Padre Pio, a saint who mysteriously bore the stigmatic wounds of Christ, used this beautiful illustration: He pictured a woman working on a piece of embroidery. Seated at his mother's feet, her little son is able to observe only the underside of her artwork. It looks like nothing more than a jumble of tangled threads. Inquisitively, he asks her what she is trying to make. Then his mother invites him to look at the upper side of her embroidery. Suddenly he is looking at a lovely picture. And, said Padre Pio, this is true in our own life. We see only the underside of our circumstances, but from a different, more transcendent perspective, it makes a picture[1]—the seen and the unseen!

There's another story I once read about a young boy who was flying his kite one day. It flew so high into the sky that cloud cover obscured it. Enveloped by the clouds, the kite completely disappeared from view.

Along came a grown man and noticed this peculiar sight: a little boy standing with a string tied around his finger, a string that went straight up in the air. "What are you doing?" the man asked the boy.

"I am flying my kite," he answered matter-of-factly.

The man looked up in the sky and stated, "I do not see any kite."

"Neither do I," said the boy.

"Then how do you know it is up there?" asked the man playfully.

The little boy answered, "Because I can feel its tug on my finger."[2]

The seen and the unseen! How do we know that this invisible God is there? Because we can feel his tug on our heartstrings!

> So we fix our eyes not on what is seen, but on what is unseen. For what is seen is temporary, but what is unseen is eternal. (2 Cor. 4:18)

Look again at the cross. There is a scene of total desolation. A would-be messiah was abandoned by his God! That is about all that any bystander could see.

> It was the third hour [9:00 a.m.] when they crucified him. The written notices of the charge against him read: THE KING OF THE JEWS. (Mark 15:25–26)

Yet this particular "king" was dying the death of a common criminal. In the book of Deuteronomy, it is stated plainly, "Anyone who is hung on a tree is under God's curse" (21:23a). Not God's blessing but His curse! So many bystanders thought that Jesus could not possibly be the Messiah.

> The chief priests and the teachers of the law mocked him among themselves. "He saved others," they said, "but he can't save himself! Let this Christ, this King of Israel, come down now from the cross, that we may see and believe." (Mark 15:31–32a)

The seen and the unseen! But there Jesus remained, pinned between heaven and earth.

> And at the ninth hour [3:00 p.m.] Jesus cried out in a loud voice, "...My God, my God, why

> have you forsaken me?"...With a loud cry, Jesus breathed his last. The curtain of the temple was torn in two from top to bottom. (Mark 15:34, 37–38)

The curtain that was torn was the one that covered the entrance to the Holy of Holies within the temple. The high priest was the only one allowed to walk through it and step into the presence of the Lord God, and he was allowed to do it only once a year. But after Jesus died, it was ripped from top to bottom (and only God could have done that), thus signaling the fact that anyone can pass through the veil to meet him. It is written in Hebrews, "We have confidence to enter the Most Holy Place by the blood of Jesus, by a new and living way opened for us through the curtain" (Heb. 10:19b–20a).

And who was the first person to walk through the torn veil? Upon his profession of faith, the Roman centurion![3] Listen to Mark's Gospel: "And when the centurion, who stood there in front of Jesus, heard his cry and saw how he died, he said, 'Surely this man was the Son of God!'" (Mark 15:39). Everyone else saw simply a dying criminal; only the centurion saw a Savior.

There is a veil before our eyes, but look hard. As the veil tears from top to bottom, you will behold the One Who says, "I am the gate; whoever enters through me will be saved" (John 10:9a).

Chapter 2

THE HIDDEN AND REVEALED

The sixth chapter of Isaiah is one of the key chapters in the Bible because it is foundational for liturgy, providing the format for worship in Jewish synagogues and Christian churches. As such, this chapter describes God's call of the prophet and moves from praise, confession, and pardon, to the proclamation of God's Word and Isaiah's dedication of himself to the Lord's service.

The chapter begins with these words: "In the year that King Uzziah died, I saw the Lord seated on a throne, high and exalted, and the train of his robe filled the temple. Above him were seraphs [perhaps the angels of God's judgment], each with six wings: With two wings they covered their faces, with two they covered their feet, and with two they were flying. And they were calling to one another: 'Holy, holy, holy is the Lord Almighty; the whole earth is full of his glory.' At the sound of their voices the doorposts and thresholds shook and the temple was filled with smoke" (Isa. 6:1–4).

The prophet, filled with amazement, finds himself looking into the throne room of heaven. I picture the whole scene filled with smoke, with the clouds of incense and the prayers of the saints (see Mal. 1:11; Rev. 5:8b, 8:3–4). In my mind's eye, I picture the Lord God being partially *hidden* and partially *revealed* in the billowing smoke of burning incense. For we serve a God who is multidimensional, a transcendent God who is both *hidden* and *revealed* at the same time. As it says in Scripture, "Truly you are a God who *hides* himself, O God and Savior of Israel" (Isa. 45:15; emphasis mine.)

As soon as we are in the presence of holiness, we immediately become aware of our own unholiness and convicted of sin. Therefore, the stunned and spellbound prophet reacted, "'Woe to me!' I cried, 'I am ruined! For I am a man of unclean lips, and I live among a people of unclean lips, and my eyes have seen the King, the Lord Almighty.' Then one of the seraphs flew to me with a live coal in his hand, which he had taken with tongs from the altar. With it he touched my mouth and said, 'See, this has touched your lips; your guilt is taken away and your sin atoned for'" (Isa. 6:5–7).

Isaiah was pardoned, but the cure was painful. I mean, having a sizzling, red-hot, fiery coal laid upon one's lips would be excruciating. But it was necessary! Do you remember when you were a child and you somehow got a cut or scrape? Your parent perhaps put iodine on the wound to cleanse and heal it. That hurt! It burned! But the hurting and the healing went together. Even so, God's redemptive touch upon our lives often brings pain in order to bring healing.

"Then I heard the voice of the Lord saying, 'Whom shall I send? And who will go for us?' And I said, 'Here am I. Send me!'" (Isa. 6:8). So this mysterious God, who keeps himself hidden from mortal eyes, revealed something of himself to Isaiah and presented him with an opportunity to respond. One poet wrote:

> Holy, Holy, Holy!
> Though the darkness hide Thee,
> Though the eye of sinful man Thy glory may not see;
> Only Thou art holy—there is none beside Thee,
> Perfect in pow'r, in love and purity.[1]

In an insightful book, *The Reason for God*, Timothy Keller was pondering mankind's ageless search for its Creator. In the course of his discussion, the author recalled a Russian cosmonaut's sarcastic comment. Upon returning to earth, he remarked that he did not see God anywhere out there. Upon hearing that, C. S. Lewis, the great Christian apologist, responded that it would be tantamount to Hamlet rummaging all over the attic in his castle, looking for Shakespeare. The playwright is *outside* the play. The only way that the playwright can be found *inside* the play is if he chooses to write himself in.[2] In short, we serve a great God who is "out of this world" and transcends our own dimension but who also reaches out to touch us. In other words, He occasionally writes himself into the play. He is a God who is both *hidden* and *revealed*. And whenever the Lord chooses to reveal himself, I believe that he reveals only what he wants us to know and only what we can understand.

In the pages of Exodus, there is an intriguing encounter between Moses and the Lord. Moses must have felt that his communication with God was entirely too indirect. He could not see the One he was talking to! My guess is that Moses wanted a face-to-face conversation. So Moses said, "'Now show me your glory.' And the Lord said, 'I will cause all my goodness to pass in front of you, and I will proclaim my name, the Lord, in your presence… But…you cannot see my face, for no one may see me and live.' Then the Lord said, '…When my glory passes by, I will put you in a cleft in the rock and cover you with my hand until I have passed by. Then I will remove my hand and you will see my back; but my face must not be seen'" (Exod. 33:18–23).

See? God *hidden* and *revealed*! God told Moses that he would see God's back but not his face. I try to picture this in my mind. I envision the Lord God partially revealing himself, passing by like a fast-moving Mack truck that is barreling along a superhighway. He would zoom by so fast that Moses would never see his grille, only His taillights! For God would hide him in the cleft of the rock and cover him with his hand. The blind poet Fanny Crosby wrote:

> A wonderful Savior is Jesus my Lord,
> A wonderful Savior to me;
> He hideth my soul in the cleft of the rock,
> Where rivers of pleasure I see.
> He hideth my soul in the cleft of the rock
> That shadows a dry, thirsty land;

> He hideth my life in the depths of His love,
> And covers me there with His hand,
> And covers me there with His hand.³

Then the Lord God came down in the cloud… And he passed in front of Moses, proclaiming, "The Lord, the Lord, the compassionate and gracious God, slow to anger, abounding in love and faithfulness…and forgiving wickedness, rebellion and sin…" Moses bowed to the ground at once and worshiped. (Exod. 34:5–8)

And so it was that the Lord God kept himself *hidden* in the cloud of his glory and yet simultaneously *revealed* himself as a loving, all-gracious God who cares for each of us. Job wrote, "When he passes me, I cannot see him; when he goes by, I cannot perceive him" (Job 9:11). We cannot get a handle on him; he gets a handle on us.

The apostle Paul knew this God who is both *hidden* and *revealed*. He wrote in 1 Timothy, "Now to the King eternal, immortal, *invisible*, the only God, be honor and glory for ever and ever" (1 Tim. 1:17; emphasis mine). And again, in that same letter, he speaks of this God "who lives in unapproachable light, whom no one has seen or can see" (6:16b). Another poet wrote, "Immortal, invisible, God only wise, In light inaccessible hid from our eyes."⁴ What God most *reveals* about himself is not simply "I AM" but "I AM HERE"—moment by moment and always present tense.

Late one night, a house caught fire and was immediately engulfed in flames. Initially it appeared that each and every family member had managed to escape—until the parents spotted their youngest son standing at a second-story bedroom window, trapped by the advancing flames. His daddy ran and stood beneath the window. Vanishing in the swirling smoke, he kept shouting, "Jump, son! Jump! I am here! I'll catch you!"

His panicky son shouted back, "But, Daddy, I can't *see* you! I can't *see* you!"

To which his father answered, "But I can see *you*!"⁵

And we rest assured in the arms of our Father God, who can see *us*.

Chapter 3

"Truth" Turned Upside Down

As we read the Bible, we begin to get the hint that God's truth frequently differs from our truth. For instance, in Isaiah it says, "'For my thoughts are not your thoughts, neither are your ways my ways,' declares the Lord. 'As the heavens are higher than the earth, so are my ways higher than your ways and my thoughts than your thoughts'" (Isa. 55:8–9). And in Romans we read, "Let God be true, and every man a liar" (Rom. 3:4a). God has a different way of seeing and judging. If your truth happens to differ from his truth, then your truth is false. In 1 Corinthians we read, "Where is the wise man? Where is the scholar? Where is the philosopher of this age? Has not God made foolish the wisdom of the world?" (1 Cor. 1:20). God turns our worldly wisdom upside down.

Our conventional wisdom says that first comes the understanding and, second, the commitment. In other words, you probably are not going to commit yourself to anything unless you first understand it. It would not make much sense to do otherwise. Do not dive into a swimming pool until you know the depth (and also if it has any water in it!).

One day a nice church couple, Bob and Kathy Dillon, visited our home. They announced that they had a little special gift for me. I would find it in our backyard. I ran to the kitchen window, and there it was—a small motorcycle. The 200 cc Honda Twin Star was all bright and shiny. I felt overwhelming gratitude, yet I was more than a little intimidated. I did not know how to ride a motorcycle and felt both thrilled and scared.

I read the instructions and tried to understand the mechanical inner workings—all to no avail! I sat on it, touched the brakes, worked the gearshift, and went nowhere. Then one day I was obliged to visit a parishioner in a nursing home in Warminster, northeast of Philadelphia. I jumped on my motorcycle and just drove it, learning as I went. That really is "flying on a wing and a prayer."

Prior to this moment, I always had believed that first comes the understanding and then the commitment, that you logically have to understand how something works before you try to work it. But sometimes the opposite is true. After all, as has been pointed out numerous times, when you walk into a room and turn on the light switch, you do not first have to understand all about electricity. Often we do not understand something without first committing ourselves to it.

This is particularly true with our spiritual life. When I was a college student, I visited a chaplain and said, "I want you to *prove* the Christian faith to me. If I understand it, then I will commit to it."

He smiled and said, "Son, I can't *prove* the Christian faith to you or to anyone else. But if you accept it, it will prove itself to you. The Christian faith has a self-authenticating validity."[1]

I figure that all of us have spiritual questions. But if we wait until they all are resolved, we never will do anything. Many of our issues will not be solved this side of death, and on the other side, we probably will not care. So do not wait until you have achieved complete understanding, or time might expire (along with you). Take that proverbial leap of faith.

It is something like this: A daddy takes his little daughter to a playground and puts her on a swing. After a few moments, he stands under the swing and says, "Jump!" He extends his arms to catch her. Now she could really spend a whole lot of time thinking about this. She could, first of all, try to comprehend the dynamics of jumping. She could try to anticipate her velocity, measure her trajectory, and figure out the timing, or she could just trust her daddy enough to let go of the swing and jump.

> The eternal God is your refuge, and underneath are the everlasting arms. (Deut. 33:27a)

First comes the commitment and then comes the understanding. Isn't that the way it is with marriage? A couple that is considering getting married begins to deal with some gnawing anxiety. If each person cannot fully understand him or herself, then how can the couple possibly understand each other? But if they delay this next step of life, they possibly could have a very long engagement. First comes the courageous act of commitment, then comes the understanding.

The Lord turns all our conventional wisdom upside down. But there are multitudes who believe that everything Jesus said is conveniently compatible with their own way of thinking. I ask myself, "What were they thinking?" Either they do not know what they are thinking, or they do not know what the Lord was thinking. Somehow, somewhere, they have misunderstood. Jesus's Sermon on the Mount goes against the grain of human nature. Much of what Jesus said seems contrary to human experience. He said, "So the last will be first, and first will be last" (Matt. 20:16). That seems backward, doesn't it? We do not think that way at all. Drive in traffic, and you will discover that in their hearts, people really believe that the first shall be first!

Again, Jesus announced to his disciples, "If anyone would come after me, he must deny himself and take up his cross and follow me. For whoever wants to save his life will lose it, but whoever loses his life for me will find it" (Matt. 16:24–25). This sounds like double-talk. But when you pause to reflect, you can see that people who have focused on acquisition instead of relationships wind up empty. Those who reach out to "grab all the gusto" might end by having full wallets and empty souls.

To expound on his point, Jesus told a little parable. A certain wealthy farmer was prospering but needed a place to store his increasingly large harvests. He thought about it and then decided that all his barns were only "tear-downs." He would get rid of them and build more monumental barns. Then when he had accumulated a whole lot of stuff, he would say with infinite self-satisfaction, "Take life easy; eat, drink and be merry." (We vainly imagine that we are in control.) "But God said to him, 'You fool! This very night your life will be demanded from you.'" Then Jesus concluded, "This is how it will be with anyone who stores up things for himself but is not rich toward God" (Luke 12:16–21).

Jesus said the opposite of what we ourselves believe: Whoever keeps, loses; whoever loses, keeps. That is our "truth" turned upside down. Jim Elliott, one of five young missionaries slain in the Amazon, once said, "He is no fool who *gives* what he cannot keep to *gain* what he cannot lose."[2] He ultimately sacrificed his earthly life to gain a heavenly one.

Here is another biblical truth that stands our human wisdom on its head. In his Sermon on the Mount, Jesus said, "Do not store up for yourselves treasures on earth, where moth and rust destroy, and where thieves break in and steal. But store up for yourselves treasures in heaven, where moth and rust do not destroy, and where thieves do not break in and steal. For where your treasure is, there your heart will be also" (Matt. 6:19–21).

One time I was solemnly intoning this passage of Scripture as I taught a class of young adults. Judy Donnelly calmly interjected, "Notice Jesus didn't say it the other way around."

"What?" I stammered.

"He didn't say, 'Where your heart is, there your treasure will be also.'" Judy smiled beatifically.

I had to think this through. Why did Jesus say it the opposite way and turn our truth upside down? Now I look at it this way: My heart is really in several marvelous charities, but is my *treasure* there? No. My treasure is in mutual funds. Is my *heart* there? You bet! See, our treasure does not always follow our heart, but our heart always will follow our treasure—guaranteed, by Jesus!

Therefore, says our Lord, be sure you put your treasure in the right place because your heart is sure to follow. It is a keen insight into our (fallen) human nature. And it turns our truth upside down.

Given a choice between human truth and God's truth, trust his. Remember the proverb: "Trust in the Lord with all thine heart; and lean not unto thine own understanding" (Prov. 3:5, KJV).

Chapter 4

TAKEN BY SURPRISE!

The Lord has a way of taking us by surprise. To illustrate this, let me share a true story about real-life people I once pastored.

Along one of the streets in a Philadelphia neighborhood were twin homes. One-half of a duplex was owned by an elderly parishioner, Edna MacNeil. A widow for several years, Edna lived alone. She was kind, gentle, good-humored, and it always was a heartwarming experience for me when I shared her company. Next door, in the other twin, was a friendly young couple. Ed and Joyce were busy raising two young sons and treated Edna as a family member. They paid a great deal of attention to her and were careful to answer her every need.

Whenever I visited Edna MacNeil, she invariably would say, "You know, Pastor, my husband and I never had any children of our own, but my next-door neighbor, Joyce, is like the daughter I never had. I just love her so much. You know what I am going to do for that family? Someday I am going to leave them my house. That way, they will own both twin homes and will have the option of renting one out or of making them into one large house by knocking out some walls or making doorways. Yes, it will be my gift to them."

Edna always included this sentiment in her conversations with me. She would leave Joyce her house. But she never did! She died without making a will. Her home subsequently was sold, and Joyce inherited nothing at all, not even a little memento. I felt sorry for Joyce and so angry with myself. I faulted myself for never asking Edna, "By the way, have you included Joyce in your *will*? Have you actually gone to an attorney? Edna, I realize that you want to leave your home to Joyce, but did you put that in writing?" These are the questions I should have asked but never did because I did not consider it my business. So Edna's home was sold because I failed to ask the crucial questions. Me? I accepted much of the blame, but I transferred most of it to the Lord. After all, he's *God*! Shouldn't he be in control of our circumstances? So I asked myself, "What was he thinking!" A completely beautiful, generous plan had gone right down the drain.

Then another young couple moved into Edna's home, Desi and Ernie. I had performed Desi and Ernie's wedding. They too were trying to raise a family. Joyce and Ed became very attached to Desi and Ernie's three children. There was an instant rapport between the two families occupying those twin homes.

All this was interrupted by a series of devastating tragedies. First, Ernie, the young father, needed a kidney transplant. Amazingly, his wife's kidney was a perfect match for a transplant, so she gave Ernie her own kidney. In less than a year, he died anyway, taking her kidney to the grave. Five years later, Desi, who had been struggling to be both mother and father to her three kids, also passed away.

Again, I asked myself, "What was he thinking?" Personally, I still do not believe that God programmed this, but at least he obviously permitted it for some reason. St. Paul once wrote, "The man without the Spirit does not accept the things that come from the Spirit of God, for they are foolishness to him, and he cannot understand them, because they are spiritually discerned" (1 Cor. 2:14). We are obliged to look more deeply at life's circumstances and see them through eyes of faith.

Three children were left orphaned. Without much in the way of family, they needed someone to be appointed as their legal guardians. Desi had already taken care of that, stipulating in her will that

Joyce and her husband were to be appointed the legal guardians. The children's mother had planned ahead.

When I visited Joyce Dence recently, I lamented my failure to ascertain that Edna MacNeil had not made a will. I expressed my regret that Joyce and Ed had lost out on owning the other twin home. "Joyce, I apologize. I should have been more intrusive, more intentional. I am sorry for the way things worked out."

She looked hard at me for a moment, then smiled and said, "Jerry, you are *sorry* for the way things worked out? Think about it! If Edna had willed us her home, then Desi and Ernie would have never moved next door. We would never have become friends. And when they died, who would have looked after their kids? Don't you see God's hand in this?"

And suddenly I did. I was nearly overwhelmed; I never had put the puzzle pieces together. I never had connected the dots. I was taken by surprise.

My mother used to tell me, "Always remember: Wherever one door closes, another will open. And God will lead you through it." In the eighth chapter of Romans—a chapter most familiar to me in the King James Version—is a passage I love to contemplate: "For as many as are led by the Spirit of God, they are the sons of God. For ye have not received the spirit of bondage again to fear; but ye have received the Spirit of adoption, whereby we cry, Abba, Father. The Spirit itself beareth witness with our spirit, that we are the children of God" (Rom. 8:14–16, KJV). So we are taken by surprise. We might not see it at first, but when we look back through eyes of faith, we see God's hand and say with Jacob in the Old Testament, "Surely the Lord is in this place; and I knew it not" (Gen. 28:16, KJV).

In a book of daily devotions, I happened upon this meditation on Israel's exodus from Egypt. The author reminded the reader that those ancient Hebrews now found themselves in a wilderness and began to long for their past. They may have been slaves in Egypt, but they also had food. In the hour of their despondency, God rained down bread from heaven upon them, giving them exactly what they needed when they needed it. He gave them manna. That word, *manna*, is actually a question that means, "What is it?" Initially, the

Hebrew people did not recognize this strange substance as God's provision for their need.[1] They were taken by surprise!

The Bible is a story of "progressive revelation." In other words, God reveals something about himself in the Old Testament. Then gradually he adds to the picture—a stroke of paint here, a stroke there. But it isn't until he sends Jesus that the picture is complete. So it is written at the beginning of Hebrews, "In the past God spoke to our forefathers through the prophets at many times and in various ways, but in these last days he has spoken to us by his Son" (Heb. 1:1–2a).

That is how God acts in your life too—like an artist. He adds a stroke here and a stroke there in your life until that picture is complete. The revelation of what he is doing, where he is doing it, and how he is doing it comes progressively over time. And it might take a while to see his finished plan.[2] Whenever we do, we are taken by surprise.

> He leadeth me: O blessed thought!
> O words with heavenly comfort fraught!
> What e'er I do, Where'er I be,
> Still 'tis God's hand that leadeth me.[3]

Chapter 5

THREE GREAT WISHES

One of the best-known tales of the *Arabian Nights* is the highly imaginative story of Aladdin's lamp. Many a child has thrilled to this fantasy. Aladdin grew up in Persia and was a lazy, shiftless boy. (I have a whole bunch like that in my own family!) But one day, quite by accident, he found himself to be in possession of a dull, unpolished brass lamp that turned out to be much more than the tarnished old relic it appeared to be. When he rubbed it, a genie magically appeared, prepared to grant his wishes. Now I do not know about you, but whenever I see some sort of dull, unpolished lamp, I am tempted to surreptitiously give it a little rub, just in case. Anyway, whenever Aladdin wished for anything, he would get it.

We all would like that: to have our secret wishes granted. In fact, that is why a lot of people come to church. They think that maybe God is the genie in the lamp who will make their every wish come true. But be careful what you wish for. You might just get it! There's the rub.

Now let's remember another story, the one about King Midas. As I recall, he wished everything he touched might turn to gold. Now he was warned to consider carefully what he was requesting. But upon his shortsighted insistence, he was granted his wish. Well, everything turned to gold, even his food and his daughter! In their selfish quests for wealth, power, and self-aggrandizement, many people have personally sacrificed their deepest relationships. So it follows that a "Midas touch" can be a curse instead of a blessing.

Let me ask you to think about this: if you could be granted three wishes, what would they be? There is a whole genre of jokes written about both wishes and their fulfillments. They always have surprise endings that take the recipient off guard. So if you could be granted three great wishes, what would they be? Most people would ask for *health*. People always say, "If you have your health, you have everything." The second wish might be for *happiness*. Once, at a wedding reception, I stood next to the bride whose wedding I had just performed. Someone came up to her and wished her "all the luck in the world," to which the bride replied—in a whining voice—"I just want to be happy!" Well, we all do. And the third great wish most of us have is *success*. We want to succeed in whatever we do. With this knowledge, you now can propose a toast at any wedding reception!

But on the night of the Last Supper, our Lord proposed a very different "toast." He offered to fulfill three great wishes that you did not even know you had. On that fateful night, Jesus said, "I am the *way* and the *truth* and the *life*. No one comes to the Father except through me" (John 14:6; emphasis mine). Here are Jesus's three great wishes for your life: that you should know and recognize the Way (the path he represents and embodies), that you should know his Truth, and that you should experience his Life. Someone wrote, "In the person of Jesus Christ there is a *way* of life that abounds in steadfast love; there is *truth*: simple, unchanging, and redeeming; and there is *life*: with power, purpose and fulfillment."[1]

First of all, Jesus plainly stated, "I am *the way.*" There are so many people who are so lost. Once I was driving with my friend Georgie Chesterton, who was acting as my navigator. As we drove, Georgie was strangely silent, and the surrounding area looked unfamiliar. Finally, I asked, "Georgie, are we lost?"

"Not at all! Somebody just misplaced our home," Georgie replied.

Many of the lost do not imagine that they are lost; somebody just misplaced their destination. It is written in Proverbs, "There is a *way* which seemeth right unto a man, but the end thereof are the ways of death" (Prov. 14:12, KJV; emphasis mine). Many of the choices that we make look good at first, but then they get us even more lost. Matthew, in his gospel, wrote this about our Lord, "But when he saw the multitudes, he was moved with compassion on them, because they fainted, and were scattered abroad, as sheep having no shepherd" (Matt. 9:36, KJV). Jesus said, "I am the Way."

Once, on the Wildwood Boardwalk, our kids (who were probably around ten years old at the time) stopped in front of one exhibit and stood there, mesmerized. I forget what it was called, maybe Space Maze, but it was basically a maze made entirely of glass. There were glass panels and mirrored panels. You paid the price of admission and then tried to maneuver through the glass labyrinth. Our niece Michelle attempted it. We watched her get lost. She made wrong turns, slammed her face into the glass panels, bumped and groped her way along, and finally wound up back at the entrance.

It is terribly painful to watch friends get lost; you feel so helpless! They naively enter the world of illicit sex, illegal drugs, and abusive relationships, and you do not know how to rescue them. Jesus says, "I am the Way!"

Once there was a traveler who got himself lost in a jungle. He found a tribesman, whom he engaged to be his personal guide. The native took a machete and hacked his way through the dense underbrush as his hitchhiker carefully followed him. Finally, the unnerved traveler cautiously asked, "Where is the path?"

His guide bluntly announced, "*I* am the path."[2]

That is what Jesus says to you. His first wish for you is that you find *the Way.*

Secondly, we need to know *his Truth.* We keep inventing our own truth. People continue to say, "All truth is relative," which is tantamount to saying, "There is no truth!"

Jesus stood before the Roman governor Pontius Pilate, who eyed his quarry warily. Pilate asked, "Are you the king of the Jews?"

Jesus simply said, "My kingdom is not of this world."

"Ah, so you're a king after all!"

Jesus answered, "For this I was born, for this I came into the world: to testify to the truth."

Pilate looked at him and cynically commented, "What is truth?" as if to say, "What good is it? I'm a politician, not a philosopher!" Then he turned and walked away from the Christ (paraphrased from John 18:33–38a).

Earlier in his ministry, Jesus had turned to the twelve and asked point-blank, "Will ye also go away?" (Remember that this was a low moment in Jesus's ministry, when all of Jesus's followers were abandoning him.)

There must have been a deafening silence. Then Simon Peter answered, "Lord, to whom shall we go? Thou hast the words of eternal life" (John 6:66–68, KJV). The words, the Truth! And this Truth does not change.

I often have come across the following illustration: There once was a music student who went to his music lesson and gave his teacher an offhand greeting, "What's the good news for today?"

His elderly mentor silently rose, crossed the room, picked up a hammer, and hit the tuning fork. As one clear note resounded throughout the room, he turned to his flippant student and informed him solemnly, "That is *A*. It's *A* today; it was *A* a thousand years ago; and it will be *A* a thousand years from now. The soprano in the upstairs studio sings off-key. The tenor next door sings flat. The piano downstairs is badly out of tune. But this, my friend," striking the tuning fork once again, "is A. And that's the 'good news' for today."[3]

The Good News is that God's truth does not change.

Thirdly, we want to know *Life*: real and authentic. Once Jesus said, "I am come that they might have life, and that they might have it more abundantly" (John 10:10b, KJV). In my personal pilgrimage through this world, I always have been looking for real life. I have discovered in my own experience that whenever I reach out to "grab all the gusto," I just bring back a handful of air. But whenever I reach out in Jesus's name to help another human being, then my own life becomes three-dimensional.

We entertain three great wishes for ourselves: *health, happiness,* and *success.* Yet unseen, standing within the shadows of our lives, is the Lord Jesus. He has three great wishes for us: that we might find the *Way,* the *Truth,* and the *Life.* Find him and you have found all three!

Chapter 6

FEAR OF THE FUTURE

Truth be told, most of us would have to admit that we are worried a lot about the future. We cannot see it. We cannot see into it. And frankly, we are afraid of it. Someone once said, "Ninety-five percent of the things we worry about never happen anyway." But that insight does not calm our fears and worries because we are afraid of getting blindsided by the other five percent!

Wouldn't you like to have a road map into the future? You could ascertain what kind of terrain you are traversing and exactly what kind of challenges you will have to face. We do not want to get blindsided; we want to be prepared for anything. Most of the time, we do not get that privilege. The future is not all neatly laid out in front of us. We just have to trust God himself to be our road map, our chart, our compass, and our GPS.

Remember the story of the twelve spies in the book of Numbers? As a result of the events in that story, the Hebrew slaves, who had made a miraculous exodus from their bondage in Egypt (where they were a conscripted labor force), now found themselves wandering aimlessly through a wilderness. They must have felt trapped between a painful past and a faceless future. All of us feel like that sometimes. The poet Matthew Arnold spoke about "wandering between two worlds, one dead, the other powerless to be born."[1]

Let's look more closely at the story of the twelve spies: "The Lord said to Moses, 'Send some men to explore the land of Canaan, which I am giving to the Israelites. From each ancestral tribe send one of its leaders.' So at the Lord's command Moses sent them out" (Num. 13:1–3a). He sent out these twelve spies to engage in reconnaissance. Among those selected were Joshua, from the tribe of Ephraim (Num. 13:8, 16), and Caleb, from the tribe of Judah (Num. 13:6). Moses gave them the following instructions: "Go up through the Negev and on into the hill country. See what the land is like and whether the people who live there are strong or weak, few or many. What kind of land do they live in? Is it good or bad? What kind of towns do they live in? Are they unwalled or fortified? How is the soil? Is it fertile or poor? Are there trees on it or not?" (Num. 13:17–20a).

"At the end of the forty days they returned from exploring the land. They came back to Moses and Aaron and the whole community...They gave Moses this account: 'We went into the land to which you sent us, and it does flow with milk and honey! Here is its fruit. But the people who live there are powerful, and the cities are fortified and very large'" (Num. 13:25–26a; 27–28a). They worked themselves into a lather of anxiety as they moved to the crescendo of their assessment: "We can't attack these people; they are stronger than we are...All the people we saw there are of great size...We seemed like grasshoppers" (Num. 13:31–33).

I have noticed something about myself. Whenever I become negative, I make everybody around me feel negative. Discouragement is not only a disease, but also it is communicable, and everyone around catches it. That is exactly what happened to those Hebrew nomads as they listened to that report: "That night all the people of the community raised their voices and wept aloud. [They] grumbled against Moses and Aaron [their leaders], and the whole assembly said to them, 'If only we had died in Egypt! Or in this desert! Why is the Lord bringing us to this land only to let us fall by the sword? Our wives and children will be taken as plunder. Wouldn't it be better for us to go back to Egypt?' And they said to each other, 'We should choose a leader and go back to Egypt'" (Num. 14:1–4).

Here they were, frozen on the spot like a deer in headlights. They were so alarmed about their future that they opted to return to the brutality of their past. That is fear of the future to the max! Then two of the twelve spies stepped forward to offer their minority report. Joshua and Caleb said, "The land we passed through and explored is exceedingly good. If the Lord is pleased with us, he will lead us into that land, a land flowing with milk and honey, and will give it to us. Only do not rebel against the Lord. And do not be afraid of the people of the land… Their protection is gone, but the Lord is with us'" (Num. 14:7–9a).

That final argument—"the Lord is with us"—should have wrapped it up. It is a clincher, an Ace of trump! A millennium later, the apostle Paul would write, "What, then, shall we say in response to this? If *God* is for us, who can be against us?" (Rom. 8:31; emphasis mine).

My guess is that most of us are more like the ten spies that offered the majority report than the two dissidents. I myself can readily identify with those fearful men who returned utterly intimidated and already defeated. Within the shadows of darkness ahead, I see giants ready to pounce. I feel like I'm just a puny grasshopper up against them. We always respond to what we see—or think we see: the giants within the shadows. What we *fail* to see is the awesome grace of a God who loves and guides us, who plans and provides for us. He is our invisible means of support!

In the inspiring Twenty-Seventh Psalm, the poet wrote, "The Lord is my light and my salvation; whom shall I fear? the Lord is the strength of my life; of whom shall I be afraid?" (Ps. 27:1 KJV). Another poet, John Greenleaf Whittier, wrote a faith-building poem that included these words:

> I know not what the future hath
> Of marvel or surprise,
> Assured alone that life and death
> God's mercy underlies…
> I know not where his islands lift
> Their fronded palms in air;

I only know I cannot drift
Beyond his love and care.[2]

One summer I was invited by Northeast Philadelphia Christian Endeavor to be their devotional speaker on a Sunday evening at their summer camp. Representing a dozen different churches, over a hundred teenagers were spending a week in worship, Bible study, and recreation at Camp Ockanickon in Medford Lakes, New Jersey. It was a lovely, woodsy setting. At nightfall, I spoke beside a large bonfire. The faces of the teenagers glowed in the firelight, and the warmth of God's love glowed in our hearts.

Later, we returned to our cabins, walking through the woods in the pitch-blackness of the night. All the teens carried flashlights, which they persisted in shining straight down the road. Their beams of light got totally lost in the enveloping darkness. It was like trying to drive your car through dense fog using your high beams. So I told them, "You are wasting your time shining your light all the way down the road. Just shine the light on the ground a few steps ahead of you. All you really need is just enough light for the next step!"

Cardinal John Henry Newman wrote:

> Lead, kindly Light, amid th' encircling gloom,
> Lead Thou me on!
> The night is dark, and I am far from home;
> Lead Thou me on!
> Keep Thou my feet;
> I do not ask to see
> The distant scene—
> One step enough for me.[3]

There once was a little boy named Roy Smith. He was deathly afraid of the dark. One night his daddy requested that he go out to the barn to retrieve some tools. When his son protested that he was scared of the dark, his father gave him a lantern. "Shine it out there in the dark. Now how far can you see?"

"Only as far as the mulberry tree!"

"Well, just go as far as that tree."
His son did that.
"Now how far can you see?"
"The henhouse!"
When he got there, his father again shouted, "Now how far can you see?"
"I can see the barn."
Step by step, guided by the light, the boy made it all the way.[4]

> Then spake Jesus again unto them, saying, I am light of the world: he that followeth me shall not walk in darkness, but shall have the light of life. (John 8:12, KJV)

Chapter 7

DOUBT AND TRUST

One day Jesus observed a crowd gathered around some of his disciples. Scribes and Pharisees were engaged in an argument with them (Mark 9:14). "'What are you arguing with them about?' he asked. A man in the crowd answered, 'Teacher, I brought you my son, who is possessed by a spirit [a demon] that has robbed him of speech. Whenever it seizes him, it throws him to the ground. He foams at the mouth, gnashes his teeth and becomes rigid'" (Mark 9:16–18a). His son was the victim of a demonic possession that was hell-bent on destroying him.

Most biblical commentators seem to conclude that the boy's symptoms describe a classic case of epilepsy. Today it is not theologically fashionable to talk about the supernatural world of the demonic. But that also is part of the "unseen," so real that it prompted this response in Scripture: "For we wrestle not against flesh and blood, but against principalities, against powers, against the rulers of the darkness of this world, against spiritual wickedness in high places" (Eph. 6:12, KJV).

It is *more convenient* to take demonic possession, voodoo, and black magic, lump them together, and dismiss the whole thing as superstition, as a quaint holdover from the biblical worldview, or automatically to assume that the boy's symptoms were the result of some sort of psychological aberration! And so we tend to rob this episode of its spiritual sizzle. However, we inadvertently continue to use terminology that subliminally alludes to the age-old belief in the reality of evil. We might say, for instance, "I don't know what *came over me!*" or "What do you suppose *got into* him to make him do that?" or "Whatever *possessed* her to act like that?" or "Something just *got hold* of him!" And each of those words/phrases points to the possibility that, deeper down in the human psyche, there is an acknowledgment of the reality of demonic possession. Many of Jesus's "miracles" were actually "exorcisms."

In any case, the poor father of the victim had approached and appealed to Jesus's disciples for help. He complained, "I asked your disciples to drive out the spirit, but they could not" (Mark 9:18b). Because Jesus's own students could not successfully expel the evil that held the boy in its grasp, Jesus himself was discredited. That is what this whole argument was really all about in the first place. The scribes and teachers of the Law saw an opportunity to pull the rug out from under Jesus's feet and make him look powerless. It is a natural conclusion: if a sports team fails to perform well, blame the coach!

> "O unbelieving generation," Jesus replied, "How long shall I stay with you? How long shall I put up with you? Bring the boy to me." So they brought him. When the spirit saw Jesus, it immediately threw the boy into a convulsion. He fell to the ground and rolled around, foaming at the mouth. (Mark 9:19–20)

Then the father begged Jesus for help, casting himself upon Jesus's compassion.

> "If you can do anything, take pity on us and help us."
> "If you can?" said Jesus. "Everything is possible for him who believes."

> Immediately the boy's father exclaimed, "I do believe; help me to overcome my unbelief!" (Mark 9:22b–24)

Is not that what we say too? "Lord, I believe; help thou mine unbelief" (Mark 9:24b KJV). All of us approach the Lord with a mixture of doubt and trust. We believe at least in part, but there is a lingering, tormenting doubt. Jesus was poised to set this father's son free, to deliver him from his demons, to usher him into a brand-new life. Yet his father was obliged to confess his personal ambivalence, his struggle between doubting and trusting.

There is a little prayer chorus that says, "Only believe, only believe; all things are possible, only believe."[1] Our doubting simply demonstrates the frailty of our humanity. Even the saints and mystics have experienced "the dark night of the soul." Great heroes of the faith have struggled through endless times of doubt: unsure about themselves, unsure about God.

For instance, I recall John the Baptist. He is one of those heroes. After all, he was the insightful prophet who stood beside the Jordan and, at the first sight of Jesus walking toward him, proclaimed, "Behold the Lamb of God, which taketh away the sins of the world" (John 1:29b KJV). I mean, he *recognized* Jesus; he could see, with spiritual discernment, that which was unseen and could not be seen by anyone else (see 1 Cor. 2:14). This was a triumph of John the Baptist's *trust*. Yet at the abortive end of his ministry—while in prison awaiting probable execution—John suddenly was consumed with *doubt*. He was so troubled and tormented that he needed an honest answer from Jesus. So he sent his own disciples to Jesus to pose this one direct question: "Are you the one who was to come, or should we expect someone else?" (Matt. 11:2–3). In response, Jesus answered, "Go back and report to John what you hear and see: The blind receive sight, the lame walk, those who have leprosy are cured, the deaf hear, the dead are raised, and the good news is preached to the poor. Blessed is the man who does not fall away on account of me" (Matt. 11:4–6).

Amidst your own doubt, do you not find yourself asking the same question? "Are you really *my* Savior, Jesus?" In the middle and the muddle of an interminably long night of depression, I asked that question, and He was there: my Savior!

From Isaiah comes this powerful affirmation of faith: "Surely God is my salvation; I will trust and not be afraid. The Lord, the Lord, is my strength and my song; he has become my salvation" (Isa. 12:2). Notice that the prophet declares, "I *will* trust." Trust goes beyond *feeling*. If it were only a feeling, then trust would come and go and be a "sometime" thing, sometimes dependent only on one's mood. But trust requires an act of the *will*, a conscious decision on your part. When you are consumed with doubt, then join the prophet and say, "I *will* trust and not be afraid." We cherish the proverb that says, "*Trust* in the Lord with all thine heart; and lean not unto thine own understanding. In all thy ways acknowledge him, and he shall direct thy paths" (Prov. 3:5–6, KJV; emphasis mine).

In his book *Perceptions*, Maxie Dunnam told a story about his own mother who, fifteen years earlier, had waged a seemingly successful battle against cancer. Now it suddenly savagely recurred. Her son was at her side in the hospital as she slowly awakened from surgery. She tried to speak, and Maxie understood that what she wanted to say was something very important to her—not trivial. When she managed to speak, she told him that when you surrender yourself to the Lord, then—no matter what happens—everything is all right. Her son understood. She was telling him that the same God who cared for her in the past is the God who would care for her now, and she could trust *him*.[2]

> Surely God is my salvation; I *will* trust and not be afraid. (Isa. 12:2; emphasis mine).

Charles Allen, in his book *Perfect Peace*, related a story about two men who were driving together. One of them was wrapped up in a crossword puzzle ("en-wrap-tured") that he assiduously was attempting to solve. He looked up and said, "I have here a three-letter word with an *O* in the middle. The clue is 'man's best friend.'"

His friend immediately suggested, "That would be *dog*."

The man doing the crossword puzzle tried it, but it did not fit. He kept studying it and said, "Well, the last letter isn't a *G*, it's a *D*."

They both remained puzzled and repeated, "Blank-*O-D*." It never occurred to either of them to try *G* as the first letter. Charles Allen commented that many people, just like those two men driving together, never manage to figure out who their best friend really is.[3]

There is a God who loves you all through your life, even though you might be unaware of his presence. "So we fix our eyes not on what is seen, but on what is unseen. For what is seen is temporary, but what is unseen is eternal" (2 Cor. 4:18). Therefore, "I will trust and not be afraid" (Isa. 12:2a).

Chapter 8

HIS EVERLASTING ARMS

There is an old evangelistic hymn that goes,

> What have I to dread, what have I to fear,
> Leaning on the everlasting arms?
> I have blessed peace with my Lord so near,
> Leaning on the everlasting arms,
> Leaning, leaning,
> Safe and secure from all alarms;
> Leaning, leaning,
> Leaning on the everlasting arms.[1]

As children of God, we can have this assurance because it is written, "The eternal God is thy refuge, and underneath are the everlasting arms." (Deuteronomy 33:27a KJV)

Deep down in our heart, each of us knows that we have been invited to lean upon the Lord, yet we find it difficult to do. One day a man carrying a heavy burden was trudging wearily along a road when another man, driving a wagon, pulled up alongside and generously offered him a ride. Gratefully the pedestrian climbed into the wagon.

After a time, the driver casually glanced over at his passenger and noticed that he was still carrying his heavy burden on his shoulders. So naturally the driver asked him why he did not simply put it down on the floorboard of the wagon. His fellow traveling companion replied that he thought he would be asking too much if he obliged his driver to carry both him and his burden too. So he figured that he would carry his own weight. Hannah Whitall Smith pointed out that, in much the same way, many Christians still stagger alone beneath their own burden. The end result is that they wind up spiritually exhausted.[2] Yet we read in the New Testament, "Cast all your anxiety on him because he cares for you." (1 Peter 5:7 NIV)

Once some missionaries were laboring to translate the Bible into an indigenous language. They were perplexed when they tried to translate the word *trust*. There seemed to be no word or phrase in the native tongue that conveyed that concept. In the midst of their puzzlement, a native, who had been assisting the team of translators, stretched out in a hammock. He casually used a phrase that meant "putting your whole weight down." Instantly they realized that they found the key phrase. Putting your whole weight down on God is the secret of trust. When we are hurt, confused, disappointed, then trusting God is like flopping down on his supportive arms.[3]

> How gentle God's commands!
> How kind his precepts are!
> Come, cast your burdens on the Lord,
> And trust his constant care.
>
> His goodness stands approved,
> Unchanged from day to day:
> I'll drop my burden at his feet,
> And bear a song away.[4]

A certain woman who had managed to overcome an extraordinary amount of adversity in her life was asked how she had done that. She answered that the Lord had borne the burden for her. Now the person who asked the question readily agreed that we certainly should take all our burdens to the Lord. The woman answered that we also must remember to leave them there. Most of us, most of the time, tend to bring our burden to him in prayer and then, after praying, we pick up the heavy weight and stagger away with it.[5]

Hannah Whitall Smith asked if you can remember just how wonderful it feels when, after a hard day's work, you simply lie down on your bed, stretch yourself out, and relax. You have leaned down with your whole weight. However, consider what would happen to your peace of mind if you were to begin to doubt your bed's ability to support you. Maybe the bed is going to collapse and dump its contents (you) onto the floor. Thinking that way is sure to spell the end of your rest and relaxation. We are enjoined to trust in his love and lean our whole weight on him.[6] For Jesus said, "Come unto me, all ye that labor and are heavy laden, and I will give you rest." (Matthew 11:28 KJV)

> As Jesus was on his way, the crowds almost crushed him. And a woman was there who had been subject to bleeding for twelve years, but no one could heal her. She came up behind him and touched the edge of his cloak, and immediately her bleeding stopped. "Who touched me?" Jesus asked. When they all denied it, Peter said, "Master, the people are crowding and pressing against you." But Jesus said, "Someone touched me; I know that power has gone out from me." put (Luke 8:42b-46 NIV)

Everyone was touching him, but this particular touch was different. Jesus knew and probably sensed the desperation that prompted that touch.

> Then the woman, seeing that she could not go unnoticed, came trembling and fell at his feet. In the presence of all the people, she told why she had touched him and how she had been instantly

healed. Then he said to her, "Daughter, your faith has healed you. Go in peace." (Luke 8:47-48 NIV)

We hear again the whisper of Jesus's words, "Come unto me, all ye that labor and are heavy laden, and I will give you rest." (Matthew 11:28 KJV) In the hauntingly beautiful hymn "Immortal Love-Forever Full," John Greenleaf Whittier inscribed these lines:

> But warm, sweet, tender, even yet.
> A present help is He…
> The healing of His seamless dress
> Is by our beds of pain;
> We touch Him in life's throng and press,
> And we are whole again.[7]

In Isaiah 26 are these words, "Thou wilt keep him in perfect peace, whose mind is stayed on thee: because he trusteth in thee." (Isaiah 26:3 KJV) At the beginning of my ministry, one of my church members shared with me this precious insight. He said, "Ever since birth each of us harbors a fear of falling. Yet, deep in my heart, I know that I can never fall into the abyss. For underneath me are his everlasting arms."[8]

Chapter 9

PERSEVERANCE

While in prison, the apostle Paul wrote a letter of encouragement to his fellow Christians in Philippi. He wanted to reassure them that he had not given up, that God had not stuck him back on the shelf, and that he was still *persevering* in his Christian walk: "I press on to take hold of that for which Christ Jesus took hold of me... Forgetting what is behind and straining toward what is ahead, I press on toward the goal" (Phil. 3:12b, 13b–14a). I press on. I *persevere*. I "break for the tape." Drop all the baggage (the fears, the grudges, the animosities) of your past. Drop everything that holds you back and run into the future to which God is calling you.

The writer of Hebrews put it like this: "Therefore, since we are surrounded by such a great cloud of witnesses, let us throw off everything that hinders and the sin that so easily entangles, and let us run with *perseverance* the race marked out for us. Let us fix our eyes on Jesus, the author and perfecter of our faith" (Heb. 12:1–2a; emphasis mine).

During the 1968 Olympics, hosted by Mexico, a dramatic episode took place. The marathon event had been won an hour earlier. The fleet-footed Ethiopian runner had finished first, completing the twenty-six-plus mile course with great exuberance. Now the sky was darkening and the air growing chilly. The remaining spectators were getting ready to exit.

Suddenly there came the commanding alarm of police sirens. Everyone turned to look toward the entrance of the stadium. A single runner named John Stephen Akhwari, bedecked in the colors of Tanzania, was entering the stadium. The very last man to finish the marathon, this injured athlete limped into the stadium, obviously struggling against crippling physical pain. He had fallen during the race but refused to quit. Determined to finish the race, he stumbled along the final four-hundred-meter track. Akhwari received an ovation almost as tumultuous as the one accorded the champion.

Considering the seriousness of his injury and the fact that he could not possibly medal, someone asked, out of curiosity, why he had continued. He answered matter-of-factly that his nation had not sent him all the way to Mexico just to *start* the race, but to *finish* it![1]

Each of us has a race to run. Some races last longer than others. Some have a hundred-yard dash, others a mile or a marathon. What counts is not how we start but how we finish. That is why St. Paul wrote, "For I am now ready to be offered, and the time of my departure is at hand. I have fought a good fight, I have finished my course, I have kept the faith" (2 Tim. 4:6–7 KJV).

There was a prophet, Jeremiah, who one day heard the Lord say, "Take a scroll and write on it all the words I have spoken to you concerning Israel, Judah and all the other nations from the [first] time I began speaking to you…till now. Perhaps…the people of Judah…. will turn from [their] wicked way; then I will forgive…their sin" (Jer. 36:2–3). The year was 605 BC when Jeremiah summoned Baruch to be his secretary, "and while Jeremiah dictated all the words the Lord had spoken to him, Baruch wrote them on the scroll" (Jer. 36:4b). Then the prophet, who was *persona non grata* with the religious establishment headquartered in Jerusalem, asked his secretary to take the scroll, go to the temple, and read it. He did just that. (Jer. 36:6, 8)

Meanwhile, the officials were privately meeting in the temple precincts, and when they discovered that the scroll of Jeremiah was being read, and *what* was being said, they probably were not amused. They sent a message to Baruch, "Bring the scroll from which you have read to the people and come." Then they said, "Sit down, please, and read it to us." And he did. As they listened, the officials were badly shaken. "We must report all these words to the king." (Jer. 36:14–16)

What made them fearful? What left them so badly shaken? The Word of God that lifts up "the down and out" and flattens "the high and mighty!" It is written in Hebrews:

> For the word of God is living and active. Sharper than any double-edged sword, it penetrates [between] soul and spirit, joints and marrow; it judges the thoughts and attitudes of the heart. Nothing in creation is hidden from God's sight. Everything is uncovered and laid bare before the eyes of him to whom we must give account. (Heb. 4:12–13)

So this scroll was not just any old scroll. It sizzled with power.

When the officials went to the king, the weather was cold and damp, "and the king was sitting in the winter apartment, with a fire burning in the firepot in front of him" (Jer. 36:22b). The blazing fire was maintained to provide warmth. Presumably, the king was warm and toasty. As he listened to the reading of the scroll, he reached over with his knife and contemptuously sliced off each column after it was read. The ribbons of the parchment fell onto the hot coals until the entire scroll was reduced to ashes. (Jer. 36:23) That was exactly the fate that awaited the Holy City—Jerusalem would be engulfed in flames.

> The king and all his attendants who heard these words showed no fear. (Jer. 36:24a)

What did they fail to hear? They heard *words*—mere *words*—but missed the *Word*! They saw the fire of *burning coals* in the firepot but missed seeing the burning fire of God's *judgment*! *The seen and the unseen!* St. Paul wrote, "So we fix our eyes not on what is seen, but on what is unseen. For what is seen is temporary, but what is unseen is eternal" (2 Cor. 4:18).

So it was that Jeremiah's entire manuscript—the work of a lifetime of prophecy—literally went up in smoke. He must have felt like quitting! Then "the Word of the Lord came to Jeremiah: 'Take another scroll and write on it all the words that were on the first scroll...' So Jeremiah took another scroll and gave it to the scribe [who] wrote on it all the words of the scroll that [the] King of Judah had burned in the fire. And many similar words were added to them" (Jer. 36:27–28a, 32). What Jeremiah *preserved* in writing survives in your Bible today, most likely as the core of the book of Jeremiah. Every Bible published today contains that scroll! In Isaiah we read, "The grass withereth, the flower fadeth: but the word of our God shall stand for ever" (Isa. 40:8, KJV). Again, he said, "So is my word that goes out from my mouth: It will not return to me empty, but it will accomplish what I desire and achieve the purpose for which I sent it" (Isa. 55:11).

Jesus one day told this little parable: "Suppose one of you has a friend, and he goes to him at midnight and says, 'Friend, lend me three loaves of bread, because a friend of mine on a journey has come to me, and I have nothing to set before him.' Then the one inside answers, 'Don't bother me. The door is already locked, and my children are with me in bed. I can't get up and give you anything.' I tell you, though he will not get up and give him the bread because he is his friend, yet because of the man's boldness he will get up and give him as much as he needs." (Luke 11:5–8) Because of his *perseverance*! (a graduate of the school of hard knocks!)

To understand this parable, we have to picture it in our minds. We must understand what kind of homes they lived in. First, the whole family generally slept in one small room. Secondly, they slept on straw mats that they spread out on the stone floor. Parents customarily slept on each end of the room, with the children sleeping between them, close together, to share the warmth. Usually their mother slept closest to the kitchen so that, without disturbing them, she could get up early in the morning to bake the bread.[2] So what you would be looking at in Jesus's homespun story is a little room filled with wall-to-wall children, all asleep. If you were their father and had to rouse yourself to heed your neighbor's call for help, you'd have to step over and between the children![3] But if the neighbor were to persevere in knocking at the door, you finally would get up and answer—not because you really wanted to help at that hour of the night but just to shut him up.

    I think that Jesus's point is that you and I serve a God who is very different and more hospitable than that householder. He is a Father who loves us and whose door is always open. Therefore, said Jesus, "Ask and it will be given to you; seek and you will find; knock and the door will be opened to you" (Luke 11:9). So never lose heart (2 Cor. 4:16a) and never become fixated on what you *see* all around you: heartache, rejection, doors slammed in your face, all those things that make you feel like quitting, like your best efforts are going up in smoke. Instead, fix your eyes on the *unseen*, on what can only be spiritually discerned: the open door, a door that opens to the very heart of God.

Chapter 10

Disappointment with Others

Jesus himself knew very well the anguish of disappointment with others. During his own life, Jesus's friends turned their backs on him. Those in whom he had invested so much time and effort and energy frequently let him down hard. According to John's gospel, there came a day when Jesus expressed his disappointment. He said, "'The words I have spoken to you are spirit and they are life. Yet there are some of you who do not believe.'…From this time many of his disciples turned back and no longer followed him. 'You do not want to leave too, do you?' Jesus asked the Twelve. Simon Peter answered him, 'Lord, to whom shall we go? You have the words of eternal life…'" (John 6:63b–64a, 66–68).

So the twelve, Jesus's core group of disciples, continued to walk with him. But one of them should have excused himself and left. Judas was rapidly losing faith in this would-be messiah. Disillusioned, he really should have dismissed himself, but he stayed to pull the whole house down. Jesus knew it already (John 6:64). He summoned his disciples together on the night of the Jewish Passover Seder, wanting to share this special moment with them, even with the one who would "do him in."

> Having loved his own who were in the world,
> he now showed them the full extent of his love.
> (John 13:1)

Judas already had struck a deal with Jesus's antagonists, selling him out for a handful of change (Matt. 26:14–16). After receiving an offering of food from his host's own hand, Judas arose from the table and scampered out into the night (John 13:30). The darkness was not only all around him, but also it was within his own heart. Jesus knew it already. His own heart followed Judas out the door. After all, the people who disappoint us the most are most often the people we love the most.

After the Seder, Jesus and his remaining followers walked to the Garden of Gethsemane, where our Lord would agonize in prayer. Suddenly, Judas was back, barging in, accompanied by a small army. Approaching Jesus, Judas put his arms around him and kissed him. "Greetings, Rabbi!"

All Jesus said was, "Friend, do what you came for" (Matt. 26:47–50).

In a prophetic psalm, these poignant words were written, "Even my close friend, whom I trusted…who shared my bread, has lifted his heel against me" (Ps. 41:9). Have you, like our Lord, ever experienced deep disappointment in someone you loved?

In 1960, when I was just twenty-three years old, I was appointed to serve two little ma-and-pa churches in the Pocono Mountains of Pennsylvania. I never had been a pastor before. I told my district superintendent, who was assigning me, "Listen. I don't yet know how to marry people or baptize people or bury people!" I was panic-stricken.

He put his arm around my shoulder and, with a big laugh, said, "Son, you'll learn."

Those two churches were only eight miles apart, yet they were separated temperamentally by light-years. Neither congregation liked the other. In retrospect, I believe this estrangement originated in a disagreement between two brothers—one was in one church, and his brother was in the other. And to top it off, their wives could not stand each other. Both families proceeded to form alliances in their respective congregations. Both churches were jealous of my time and attention. The only way to resolve it was to "cut the pastor in half" (reference to the story told in 1 Kings 3:16–28).

Well, I preached on the Sermon on the Mount in a desperate attempt to show them another way of life. I might as well have been preaching in Aramaic. I could neither dissuade them nor disabuse them of their accusations and recriminations against each other.

Then our two feuding churches received a God-given opportunity: the offer of free land to build *one* church. The parcel of land was located exactly between the two congregations. I had such high hopes! We could construct one church building, become one congregation, pool our resources, reconcile, and reach out to others with that same spirit of love and acceptance.

The two congregations eventually distanced themselves from my vision, voting down the proposal. To them, it was tantamount to inviting a leper to share your bath! I was so bitterly disappointed in my parishioners. I was reminded of Jesus's lament, "Why do you call me, 'Lord, Lord,' and do not do what I say?" (Luke 6:46).

Disappointment with others—if you are human, you have experienced it too. However, it is important to recognize that not only have we been disappoin*ted*, but also we have been disappoin*ters*. I read the following story: A United States marine, just out of combat, returned to San Francisco and contacted his well-to-do, socialite mother in New York City. He explained to her that he would be bringing home with him a serviceman who had lost his arm and his leg in combat. He then asked if this would be upsetting to her.

His mother informed him that she would be very much upset if he were to do that. She said that someone injured to that extent would demand a lot of extra care and attention, which she was too busy to offer. Furthermore, she wondered what her social peers would think if they learned that she was supplying hospitality to someone that defective! And on top of that, didn't her son realize how inconvenient it would be? The young man replied that he completely understood her position. A couple of days later, he took his own life. You see, *he* was the one who had lost his arm and leg.[1]

Disappointment with others! We all have experienced it. How do you respond? How *should* you respond? We usually try to withdraw from those who have hurt us so that we will not be hurt even more. Yet far back in the pages of the Old Testament, back in the book of Genesis, there is an instructive story about a young man named Joseph. God placed that story in the Bible because there is something he wants us to hear with the "third ear," and see with the "third eye."

The story begins: "Now [Jacob] loved Joseph more than any of his other sons, because he had been born to him in his old age; and he made a richly ornamented robe for him. When his brothers saw that their father loved him more than any of them, they hated him and could not speak a kind word to him" (Gen. 37:3–4). One day, when the brothers were out in the fields with their flocks, Joseph came out to see them. They saw him coming and immediately began hatching a plot—"Let's just kill him and dump his body into one of the cisterns. We'll say that a wild animal ate him" (Gen. 37:17b–20). They themselves couldn't "swallow" him, yet they did not want his blood on their hands, so they scaled down their plan for vengeance by just stripping him of his high-fashion robe and throwing him alive into the cistern (Gen. 37:23–24). Talk about feeling let down by your loved ones! Talk about being disappointed with others! This was the pits!

Eventually his brothers had a slight twinge of conscience. Seeing a bunch of merchants in a caravan, they sold their brother to them (Gen. 37:25–28). (Have *you* ever felt "sold out" by someone you trusted?) Because of his brothers' treachery, Joseph was dragged through one tribulation after another. He eventually would wind up in prison. There, you would imagine, he would spend all his time plotting sweet revenge, but he didn't. Whatever his future, it was in God's hands. Joseph focused not on *disappointment*; he fixed his eyes on His appointment.

Years later, during a time of famine in the Middle East, Joseph's brothers came down to Egypt, hoping to purchase grain. They promptly were escorted into the presence of the governor, who was—guess who? They did not recognize him, but Joseph recognized them (Gen. 42:6–8). Surely, this was Joseph's opportunity to avenge himself, but he did not take it. He played a few mind games with them. Then finally he could not stand the tension any longer and revealed—amidst his sobs—his identity. He said, "'I am Joseph! Is my father still living?' But his brothers were not able to answer him, because they were terrified at his presence." He repeated his disclosure, "I am your brother Joseph, the one you sold into Egypt…do not be angry with yourselves for selling me here, because it was to save lives that God sent me ahead of you" (Gen. 45:1–7). He continued, "You intended to harm me, but God intended it for good" (Gen. 50:20a).

When others let you down, look beyond your disappointment to *his* appointment—the seen and the unseen!

> So we fix our eyes not on what is seen, but on what is unseen. For what is seen is temporary, but what is unseen is eternal. (2 Cor. 4:18)

Behind the circumstances of our lives is the invisible hand of God, a God who says, "'Never will *I* leave you; never will *I* forsake you.' So we say with confidence, 'The Lord is my helper; I will not be afraid'" (Heb. 13:5b–6a, quoting Deut. 31:6, 8 and Ps. 118:6).

Chapter 11

"Disappointment with God"[1]

One day I received a phone call from my cousin in Florida. I had not heard from him in years, but suddenly, here was Bob Allesandrini on the other end of the phone.

"I'm glad to hear your voice, Bob. It's been a few years! How's everything going?"

There was a long pause. Then he said, "I'm afraid I don't have very good news." He started to sob. "Our son, Dean, was killed last night on his way home from work. He left behind a wife and three children, ages ten, eight, and six."

I felt a shockwave thunder through my heart. "What happened?"

"He was riding his motorcycle. Suddenly, and without warning, a truck that was coming toward him made a left-hand turn right in front of him. Apparently, the other driver just didn't see him. Dean had no chance. To avoid a collision, my son laid his bike down, and the driver behind him ran over him. He's gone, Jerry, he's gone!"

Bob and his family had trusted the Lord so completely! How could God have permitted this to happen?

There undoubtedly have been terrible moments in your life when you have felt let down by God. When I entered the ministry in July of 1960, I met a woman in her seventies named Carrie Gardner. One day she tearfully shared with me an agonizing moment from her distant past. Back then, her three-year-old daughter was the light of her life. This little girl really connected with the deliveryman, who stopped at her home each day to deliver bread. He would always make a big fuss over her.

One day he stopped, laughed, and chatted with her a while, and then he backed his truck out of the driveway. Unbeknown to him, the little girl had run behind his truck, and without realizing it, he had inadvertently backed over her. This little package of joy now lay crumpled and dead. Her mother, a faithful Christian and church attendee, was now and forever disappointed with God.

Isaiah also felt disappointed with God. Why did not God intervene in critical situations? Why did he remain silent? Invisible? Motionless? Inert? Why didn't he *do* something!

> Oh, that you would rend the heavens and come down, that the mountains would tremble before you! As when fire...causes water to boil, come down...and cause the nations to quake before you! (Isa. 64:1–2)

Come down here and *do* something! Just tear up the firmament, shred the fabric of the sky, throw around some lightning bolts, and get involved in our lives!

But then again, Lord, maybe it is not that *you* have abandoned us; maybe *we* have abandoned you. We have to acknowledge our own guilt, for we indeed are sinful creatures. So Isaiah continues, "All of us have become like one who is unclean, and all our righteous acts are like filthy rags; we all shrivel up like a leaf, and like the wind our sins sweep us away. No one calls on your name...Yet, O Lord, you are our Father. We are the clay, you are the potter; we are all the work of your hand" (Isa. 64:6–8).

We get frustrated with the Lord because he does not always *intervene* to heal our loved one or to prevent an accident that is about to happen. We think that either he *can't* or he *won't*. So we are stuck in that age-old dilemma: either God lacks the *power* to change the outcome, or else he lacks the *will*. Then your choice is reduced to either having a God who is powerless or having a God who does not care. But this simplistic choice is illusory to begin with. Behind all that we can *see* is the invisible hand of God. We are the clay; He is the Potter. We are all the work of his hand.

When the Hebrew people were slaves in Egypt, the Lord God sent Moses to the Pharaoh, commanding him to release this people from their captivity—"That same day Pharaoh gave this order to the slave drivers and foremen in charge of the people: 'You are no longer to supply the people with straw for making bricks; let them go and gather their own straw. But require them to make the same number of bricks as before; don't reduce the quota…'…The Israelite foremen appointed by Pharaoh's slave drivers were beaten…'Why didn't you meet your quota of bricks yesterday or today, as before?'" (Exod. 5:6–8a, 14)

Now these Israelite foremen, who had been unjustly beaten by the Egyptians, came after Moses and his brother, Aaron, and said to them accusingly, "'You have made us a stench to Pharaoh and his officials and have put a sword in their hand to kill us'" (Exod. 5:20–21). In other words, you have given them the excuse! They accused Moses of meddling in their lives and making everything worse. Instead of blaming Pharaoh, they took everything out on Moses, blaming *him* for their predicament.

And what did Moses do? He turned around and blamed the whole thing on God. Have you ever done that?

> Moses returned to the Lord and said, "O Lord, why have you brought trouble upon this people? Is this why you sent me? Ever since I went to Pharaoh to speak in your name, he has brought trouble upon this people, and you have not rescued your people at all." (Exod. 5:22–23)

You have not rescued your people! That is major disappointment with God!

Moses was disappointed with God—because he was unable to see the Divine Plan. We tend to respond only to what we can see, not to what we cannot see. Moses responded to the human *predicament*, not to God's *presence*. The drama of the Exodus was about to begin. John Greenleaf Whittier wrote:

> I know not what the future hath
> Of marvel or surprise,
> Assured alone that life and death
> God's mercy underlies.
> …I know not where his islands lift
> Their fronded palms in air;
> I only know I cannot drift
> Beyond his love and care.[2]

An evangelist, Ron Susek, once came to a church I pastored and presented a seminar entitled "Discovering the Real You."[3] As I recall, he explained that "the real you" happens to be a sinner in need of God's grace. Then he shared with us a shrewd insight that went something like this: We look all around us and see genuine pain and suffering. We wonder why God permits it. But I personally do not think it is his business to go around stopping pain or preventing these things from happening. Instead, it is his purpose to use suffering creatively in order to "shape us up"—to shape us into the image of his Son.

Susek continued and said that he realized people like to quote Romans 8:28: "And we know that all things work together for good to them that love God, to them who are the called according to his purpose" (KJV). You probably love quoting that verse yourself. But never quote it without adding the next verse: "For whom he did foreknow, he also did predestinate to be conformed to the image of his Son" (Rom. 8:29a, KJV) God wants you to be more like Jesus and often uses the painful and disappointing experiences in your life to transform you into Christ's image.

Ron Susek's insight presented a different *perspective*. All we can see, all we are aware of, is our obvious disappointment. What we cannot see are God's plan, God's purpose, and God's providence in our lives; what we cannot see is the invisible hand of the Potter upon our mortal clay.

> "So we fix our eyes not on what is seen, but on what is unseen. For what is seen is temporary, but what is unseen is eternal." (2 Cor. 4:18)

I will never forget the story of a woman in my church. Ava Irons was a resident in a retirement home in Ephrata, Pennsylvania. Ever since her early teens, she had suffered with poor health and depression. I never figured out if the depression created the poor health or the poor health created the depression, or if they occurred concurrently. Now, in her late seventies, she was dealing with afflictions like neuropathy, osteoporosis, etc. One day she heard about a Benny Hinn Healing Service that was scheduled for the Convention Center in Philadelphia. Here was a glitzy, glittering miracle extravaganza "coming to a location near you!" She desperately wanted me to take her there. Excitedly, she said, "Oh, Pastor, I have such faith. I just know that if I go there, the Lord has promised to heal me. I believe that with all my heart!" So I arranged to take her.

We sat in a super-charged atmosphere of prayer and praise and witnessed, with our own eyes, people being healed. Ava was not healed; her legs were still crippled in spite of the chorus of "Praise the Lord!" and "Thank you, Jesus!" all around us. Sitting forlornly next to her, I could hear her asking herself, "When is it *my* turn?!" I could feel her growing disappointment with God. Around 10:00 p.m., she said very flatly, "Pastor, I think I'd like to go home now."

All the way home I shared her depression. The Lord had been there. The Holy Spirit obviously had been moving through the auditorium, but for some reason, He had not touched *her*. I gently suggested that whenever we come to the Lord in prayer, we might not receive what we ask for specifically, but we will always receive a blessing. So I told her to keep her eyes open, to fix them on the unseen, to watch and see.

When I returned to see her a week later, she was radiant, glowing with joy. "Pastor, I'm still crippled, still in pain. But remember how I told you that I used to write religious poetry? Then I eventually lost the inspiration and wasn't able to write anything. For years I've written nothing. Well, shortly after attending the healing service, I was sitting in a corner in my wheelchair when suddenly a flood of poetry came into my mind, and I automatically began to write it down!" She was writing inspired poetry!

We get disappointed with God because—with our mortal eyes—we cannot see the Divine Plan. Ava plainly had come to him in faith. He did not heal her legs. He did not heal her back. He did not heal her neuropathy. He did not heal her osteoporosis. He healed her soul.

Chapter 12

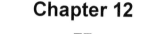

FAITH IN SPITE OF

Sometimes we face trying circumstances, and all our spiritual props suddenly are knocked out from under us. We are left unsure about the validity of our faith and without any visible or invisible means of support. We want to believe, and we struggle to believe, but we cannot quite make it. Like the father of that afflicted boy, we say, "Lord, I believe; help thou mine unbelief" (Mark 9:24b, KJV).

If that ever has been your experience, if you ever have been tempted to chuck your faith, then you can identify with the feelings of the psalmist who challenged God's seeming indifference to the sufferings of the innocent. Throughout his lamentation, the psalmist raved, ranted, and raged yet finally concluded with a ringing affirmation of faith, "*Nevertheless* I am continually with thee…Thou shalt guide me with thy counsel, and afterward receive me to glory. Whom have I in heaven but thee? And there is none upon earth that I desire beside thee…My heart and my flesh faileth: but God is the strength of my heart, and my portion forever" (Ps. 73:23–26, KJV; emphasis mine)

That is what I mean by *"faith in spite of…"* It is a faith that goes on believing *in spite of* anything and everything. Marva Dunn, a woman who is both a prominent church musician and theologian, wrote autobiographically that she continually has endured a barrage of physical afflictions: cancer, immune deficiency, and loss of mobility in her arms and legs. All during these struggles, she has experienced a loss of control and tried to retrieve it. She came to realize that all her efforts to maintain control of her life were contrary to God's control of her life. She was working at cross-purposes with His will. She recognized that she needed to surround herself with people who just let God be God. She concluded that whenever we can praise God no matter what else is happening in our lives, we are demonstrating the "nevertheless" principle. We are affirming the grace of God.[1] That is *faith in spite of!*

How can we go on believing *in spite of* whatever is going on in our lives? Because we never can be separated from God's love! That is precisely why the apostle Paul could write,

> What then shall we say to these things? If God be for us, who can be against us? …Who shall separate us from the love of Christ? Shall tribulation, or distress, or persecution, or famine, or nakedness, or peril, or sword?…Nay, in all these things we are more than conquerors through him that loved us. For I am persuaded, that neither death, nor life, nor angels, nor principalities, nor powers, nor things present, nor things to come, nor height, nor depth, nor any other creature, shall be able to separate us from the love of God, which is in Christ Jesus our Lord. (Rom. 8:31, 35, 37–39)

That, for sure, is *faith in spite of!*

There have been many Christians who have suffered through critical surgeries, the tragic loss of loved ones, failed relationships, and deep disappointments—and who still retained their faith. Every crisis is a rock on which the faith of some has been shattered and the faith of others has been built up. The prophet Habakkuk wrote, "Though the fig tree does not bud and there are no grapes on the vines, though the olive crop fails and the fields produce no food, though there are no sheep in the pen and no cattle in the stalls, yet I will rejoice in the Lord, I will be joyful in God my Savior" (Hab. 3:17–18). He chose to rejoice no matter what storms—or *floods*—came!

Again, recall with me the haunting image of Christ walking on the water. His followers were adrift on *a storm-tossed sea*. At the very moment of their complete unraveling, he came to them. They had been relying on their own street smarts, just like we do! But all at once, Jesus was there. Presumably, this was not the dirty, sweaty, earthly rabbi they had been traipsing after, but the Eternal, Cosmic Christ. Simon Peter asked Jesus to summon him to himself, "Bid me come to you," and when Jesus did, Simon Peter took his first feeble, faltering steps toward his Lord (Matt. 14:24–29). Have faith that in your storms Jesus will be there.

Clarence Macartney illustrated the scene this way. He asked if you yourself are able to walk on water. He said that you know you can walk on *land*, but can you walk on *water*? Are you able to walk on the sea of loneliness, despair, sickness, or temptation? Can you walk upon those troubled seas? You indeed can, if you want to—not trusting in yourself but trusting in *him*! You have to make the same request that Simon Peter made when he said, "Bid me come to you" (Matt. 14:28). Whenever you choose to make such a prayer, he'll say, "Come" (Matt. 14:29a).[2]

Charles Wesley wrote:

> Jesus, lover of my soul,
> Let me to thy bosom fly,
> While the nearer waters roll,
> While the tempest still is high.
> Hide me, O my Savior hide,
> Till the storm of life is past;
> Safe into the haven guide;
> O receive my soul at last.[3]

When you walk through the storm or flood or *fire*, the Lord will be with you. In Isaiah we find this promise:

> But now, this is what the Lord says: "Fear not, for I have redeemed you; I have summoned you by name; you are mine. When you pass through the waters, I will be with you; and when you pass through the rivers, they will not sweep over you. When you walk through *fire*, you will not be burned; the flames will not set you ablaze. For I am the Lord, your God, the Holy One of Israel, your Savior." (Isa. 43:1–3a, emphasis mine)

In his thought-provoking book *When God Doesn't Make Sense*, Dr. James Dobson noted three men who were obliged to walk through fire. In the third chapter of Daniel, his three friends incurred the king's anger by their steadfast refusal to worship an idol. The penalty for this refusal was incineration in a fiery furnace. Unconvinced, Shadrach, Meshach, and Abednego pursued their defiant course and said, "If we are thrown into the blazing furnace, the God we serve is able to save us from it, and he will rescue us from your hand, O king. But even if he does not, we want you to know, O king, that we will not serve your gods or worship the image of gold you have set up" (Dan. 3:17–18). That is *faith in spite of*. Even if God chose not to rescue them, they still would serve him anyway. So, said Dobson, we too know that our God is able to heal disease, handicaps, and hardships. But no matter what happens, we will keep on trusting.[4]

And when the king looked into the fiery furnace, he saw not three men but *four*, and the fourth was like the Son of God (Dan. 3:25, KJV). Only the original three condemned men emerged from the fire, so where is the fourth man? He is still there—ready to comfort you when *you* walk through fire.[5] The king peered into the blazing furnace and could see the *unseen*. In your own fiery trials, can you?

Chapter 13

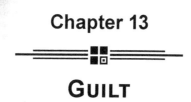

GUILT

When any of us are actively engaged in child care and we are sitting at the kitchen table beside a toddler who is attempting to feed himself and looks a lot like someone who just threw all his food into an electric fan, we might say to him reassuringly, "That's okay. Everybody spills!" Certainly that is true with human nature. We all spill; we all mess up. The Bible clearly states, "For all have sinned and fall short of the glory of God" (Rom. 3:23).

One of the most beautiful psalms ever written is the penitential Psalm 51. The psalmist begins with this prayer, "Have mercy on me, O God, according to your unfailing love; according to your great compassion blot out my transgressions" (Ps. 51:1) Like the biblical poet, we recognize and acknowledge our profound sin. We cannot minimize it, rationalize it, fix it, or explain it away. We have nowhere else to go but up. We cast ourselves on God's mercy and trust in his steadfast love.

The psalmist continues, "Wash away all my iniquity and cleanse me from my sin. For I know my transgressions, and my sin is always before me" (Ps. 51:2–3). By now, our sin is so apparent to us that it is constantly in our face. We ask God to wash us clean, feeling dirty on the outside and filthy deep within. We need to be cleansed from the inside out.

The prophet Isaiah wrote, "'Come now, let us reason together,' says the Lord. 'Though your sins are like scarlet, they shall be as white as snow; though they are red as crimson, they shall be as wool'" (Isa. 1:18). What a promise! In the midst of our "bad news," here is the *good news*. Sung to an American folk melody is the hymn:

> There is a fountain filled with blood
> Drawn from Immanuel's veins,
> And sinners plunged beneath that flood
> Lose all their guilty stains...
> The dying thief rejoiced to see
> That fountain in his day,
> And there may I, though vile as he,
> Wash all my sins away.[1]

I remember a time in my life (certainly not *the* time *of* my life!) when I got a job as a handyman at a hotel on Cape Ann (East Gloucester), Massachusetts. It was August of 1959. When I applied for this summer job, my potential employers eyed me up and down carefully and then asked with suspicion, "Well, what can you do?"

With more courage than brains, I cavalierly replied, "Everything." That bold answer was embarrassingly far from the truth. I proceeded to make a mess in whatever area I found myself.

Finally, exasperated, they asked me to paint the ceiling over a long hallway. "You ever painted before?" they asked.

"Of course," I blithely answered. They went away and left me alone (their second mistake!). I looked at the ceiling, the can of paint, and the brush and concluded that this project was fairly uncomplicated. All I had to do was put the paint on the ceiling.

First, I started at the wrong end of the hallway, and I literally painted myself into a corner. It was a tactical blunder. Secondly, I never put newspaper down on the floor because I never envisioned the paint dropping from the ceiling like pennies from heaven. It was not my fault; gravity was entirely to blame. The paint dripped down onto a rubber floor mat. When I attempted to clean it up with some sort of solvent, the rubber melted. Now I found myself crawling through dirt, paint, solvent, and melted rubber.

One of my bosses appeared at the doorway and just stared, frozen in time. There was a look of revulsion on his face. I asked, pathetically, "Whose shower can I use?" (I did not have access to a shower.)

Curling his lip in sheer disgust, he answered in one word, "Nobody's!"

In that single timeless moment, I was convinced that I would spend the remainder of my natural life all covered with paint and melted rubber.

Isn't that our spiritual condition? We get covered in our own grime and ask, "Whose shower can I use? How can I get cleaned up?" And there is no door opening for us. We cannot go anywhere else to get rid of our stains. There is no one who can do that for us. With all our guilt, there is nowhere else to go but up. "And there may I, though vile as he, wash all my sins away."[2]

Something in my past that brought me infinite guilt was my father's death. I really never can forgive myself for my own inaction. He was eighty years old and battling a blood disease. Because his immune system had been severely compromised and he had virtually no resistance, he came down with a virus. When my mother informed me about his condition, I concluded that it seemed non-life threatening. (That turned out to be wrong.) Though my parents lived only nine miles away, I did not stop in to see him. I spent time calling on numerous parishioners, but I neglected to see him. Once I made a pastoral call at Einstein Hospital and, on my way home, passed within two blocks of his house. But I did not stop in and see him!

After he died—that very day—my mother was remembering, in vivid detail, the last week of his life. She casually commented that one day my dad, who was lying in the front bedroom, heard a car pull up and someone get out. "It must be Jerry," he said with great anticipation. It must be, but it was not. Then a few days later, this man, who always had taken care of me, died. Now where do I go with that? Where do I take my guilt? There is nowhere else but up.

With the psalmist I have to confess, "Against you, you only, have I sinned and done what is evil in your sight" (Ps. 51:4a).

How can I say, "Against you, you *only* have I sinned?" Because any sin against anyone is ultimately against God! The buck stops there! Listen to what our Lord tells us in Matthew 25:

> Then he [the King] will say to those on his left, "Depart from me, you who are cursed, into the eternal fire prepared for the devil and his angels. For I was hungry and you gave me nothing to eat, I was thirsty and you gave me nothing to drink, I was a stranger and you did not invite me in, I needed clothes and you did not clothe me, I was sick and in prison and you did not look after me…I tell you the truth, whatever you did not do for one of the least of these, you did not do for me." (Matt. 25:41–43, 45b)

So we come to this One against whom our sin ultimately is directed and say, "Cleanse me with hyssop, and I will be clean; wash me, and I will be whiter than snow" (Ps. 51:7). I cannot possibly wash myself clean, and I know it. On the night of what came to be called the Last Supper, Jesus knelt before the feet of a recalcitrant Simon Peter and said, "Unless I wash you, you have no part with me." I am like Peter when he answered, "Then, Lord, not just my feet but my hands and my head as well" (John 13:8b–9). When there is nowhere else to go but up, we look up to "him who is invisible" (Heb. 11:27b)—unless seen through eyes of faith!

There is an instructive story about Jesus's forgiveness, a story told in Mark 2. Jesus entered his Galilean headquarters, the village of Capernaum. When the townspeople heard that he had come home, they mobbed his house. Not only was there no room inside, but also there was no room outside. Jesus preached to them. He was playing before a packed house. Then a group of men arrived bearing a paralyzed man on a litter (Mark 2:1–3). They lugged their patient to the roof of the house, most likely up an outside staircase. Then they made a hole in the roof and lowered the litter down, depositing the crippled man right at the feet of Jesus (Mark 2:4). It gives new meaning to the expression "dropping in on someone"!

Now here was this paralytic, lying flat on the ground. There is one good thing about being laid out flat: you have to look up. There is nowhere else to look but up. He was looking into the face of Jesus.

When Jesus realized the faith of the men who had brought him, he looked at their patient and said, "Son, your sins are forgiven" (Mark 2:5). Jesus already had diagnosed his problem. Today we might say it was psychosomatic. It was guilt that was crippling him. The heart of the matter was the matter of the heart. Therefore our Lord did not say, "Your legs are fixed." He said instead, "Your sins are forgiven."

Jesus can exercise that same power in your life today. He looks at you, through you, into you and says, "My son, my daughter, your sins are forgiven."

> Just as I am, without one plea,
> But that thy blood was shed for me,
> And that thou bidst me come to thee,
> O Lamb of God, I come, I come!
>
> Just as I am, and waiting not
> To rid my soul of one dark blot,
> To thee whose blood can cleanse each spot,
> O Lamb of God, I come, I come![3]

When there is nowhere else to go, we go to him.

Chapter 14

TRIALS

A blind poet, Fanny Crosby, wrote,

> All the way my Savior leads me;
> What have I to ask beside?
> Can I doubt His tender mercy,
> Who through life has been my Guide?...
>
> All the way my Savior leads me,
> Cheers each winding path I tread,
> Gives me *grace for every trial*,
> Feeds me with the living bread...[1]

"Grace for every trial!" The Lord had guided this blind poet with each step she had taken in the dark, and this is the same Lord who will guide *you* in the ultimate "trust walk." It is written in the forty-third chapter of Isaiah, "When you pass through the waters, I will be with you; and when you pass through the rivers, they will not sweep over you. When you walk through the fire, you will not be burned; the flames will not set you ablaze. For I am the Lord, your God, the Holy One of Israel, your Savior" (Isa. 43:2–3a). He is with you through your trials.

One the most stressful trials you will endure is *sickness*. So many times I have stood at the bedside of a critically ill patient and privately wondered how to pray or what to pray. As a hospital chaplain, I often have stood beside a patient who was being "extubated," removed from life support. I mentally would search my mind and ransack the spiritual filing cabinet in my brain for just the right prayer. I would think, *Do I pray for this person to die or to get better?*

One day I was having lunch at a diner in the Mayfair neighborhood of Philadelphia. I was sitting across the table from a Baptist pastor, Carl Swansen. As we were eating, I casually asked this question, "Carl, whenever you're ministering to someone who is between life and death, how do you pray? I mean, what do you say? What do you ask God?"

He sat there contemplatively and then said, "There's a passage in Scripture where Jesus is anticipating his own death. It's found in the twelfth chapter of John." He reached into his suit coat pocket and whipped out a pocket Bible. Opening it, he flipped through the pages until he came to it. "Here it is: 'Now is my soul troubled; and what shall I say? Father, save me from this hour: but for this cause came I unto this hour. Father, glorify thy name' [John 12:27–28a, KJV]

"You know," he continued, "Whenever I'm with a parishioner who is lying there between life and death and I honestly don't know whether I should be praying for the Lord to heal him or to take him home, I remember Jesus's prayer. I just pray that prayer, 'Father, glorify thy name' [John 12:28a, KJV]. In other words—that the Lord will be glorified either way! He will be glorified in the wonderful way this person confronts death or in his miraculous recovery. Either way: 'Father, glorify thy name.'"

In 1 Peter, the apostle expressed this same hope: "You may have had to suffer grief in all kinds of trials. These have come so that your faith...may be proved genuine and may result in praise, glory and honor when Jesus Christ is revealed. Though you have not seen him, you love him; and even though you do not see him now, you believe in him and are filled with an inexpressible and glorious joy" (1 Pet. 1:6b–8)—the seen and the unseen!

The founder of the Salvation Army, General William Booth, struggled with failing eyesight as he aged. Finally, his son was obliged to tell him that the progress of his ocular disease was irreversible and irrevocable. Eventually he would be totally blind. His father absorbed the news and then commented philosophically, "Son, all my life I've served the Lord *with* my eyesight. For the rest of my life I'll serve the Lord *without* my eyesight."[2] Either way, he would serve the Lord, who would be glorified. St. Paul wrote, "Now to the King eternal, immortal, invisible, the only God, be honor and glory for ever and ever" (1 Tim. 1:17a).

As I said, one of the most stressful trials that we endure is *sickness*. Another is *rejection*. The feeling of rejection easily can fold us up and trash us. Dr. John Sutherland Bonnell, pastor of the prestigious Fifth Avenue Presbyterian Church in New York City, had the well-deserved reputation of being a superb pastoral counselor. In the pastor's study, he displayed a painting of Hofmann's *Christ in Gethsemane* (the picture of Jesus kneeling in prayer in the Garden of Gethsemane). Many who came to him for counseling commented on the picture. He later remarked how much it resonated with those who sought his counsel.

He offered an illustration. One day a very angry, bitter woman came to him, raging against the long record of injustices perpetrated against her. She was incensed not only by those who had done these things but also by the God who had permitted them. She avenged herself by discontinuing Bible study and church attendance. For two years she had not attended worship. The pastor let her blow off steam, all the while noticing that she kept glancing at the painting of Jesus.

Dr. Bonnell unobtrusively moved his chair so that they both could look at the painting. Counselor and counselee sat side by side, silently reflecting. Finally, the pastor broke the silence by suggesting that life indeed had been difficult for her. "Yes," she nodded. He then made the observation that life had not been very easy for Jesus either. Again, she nodded in agreement. Then he asked her, pointedly, why she thought the artist had painted a thorn bush beside the rock where Jesus was kneeling in prayer. She supposed that it was an allusion to the crown of thorns he would be forced to wear on the cross. Next he asked about the sleeping disciples. She thought they served as a reminder that his closest friends, on whom he depended, would let him down when he most needed them. Yes, she knew how he must have felt.[3]

At that point Dr. Bonnell asked her how she could explain Jesus's victory over his circumstances, his triumph over his trials. She focused intently on the painting and found the answer in the picture itself. It was self-explanatory. Jesus was kneeling in *prayer*, a connection that afforded him the strength to endure. The pastor then asked her to consider that the same God would do the same thing for her.

She thought about that and gradually saw herself with greater clarity. She realized that her self-absorption and bitterness had exacerbated her circumstances, alienating her friends and isolating her from their support. In other words, she began to see her own complicity. In that moment of new self-awareness, the pastor gently suggested that the two of them pray. In her heartfelt prayer, she unburdened herself and repented, discovering a deep joy that never would fade away.[4]

Each of us certainly will face many trials in our lifetime. We see our problems but not his presence. He does not remove all our trials. Instead, he is with us through them, whispering, "I Am Here!"

> All the way my Savior leads me,
> Cheers each winding path I tread,
> Gives me grace for every trial,
> Feeds me with the living bread…[5]

Chapter 15

THE NEED TO FORGIVE

One day "Peter came to Jesus and asked, 'Lord, how many times shall I forgive my brother when he sins against me? Up to seven times?' Jesus answered, 'I tell you, not seven times, but seventy times seven.'" (Matthew 18:21-22 NIV, with an alternative reading for verse 22) Let us think about that for a minute. That equation adds up to 490. So we have to tell ourselves, "488, 489, 490. I have reached my limit." Using Near Eastern hyperbole, Jesus made the point that one would soon lose count. That is what Jesus is telling you today: continue to forgive until you lose count. We are told in the great chapter on love, 1 Corinthians 13, that love "keeps no record of wrongs." (1 Corinthians 13:5b NIV)

To illustrate this, Jesus shared a story about a king who decided to settle his accounts and to call in the money that was owed to him. One of his debtors owed a huge debt that seemed impossible to repay. I imagine that he was not even able to pay the interest, let alone the principal. The king therefore ordered that the debtor's entire household be liquidated. This poor man dropped to his knees and implored the king, "Just give me some more time, and I'll repay in full." The king observed this display of abject remorse and decided to forgive the debt and let him off the hook.

Upon his release, this forgiven debtor went and found a man who owed him a relatively small amount. His creditor now demanded immediate repayment. The man begged for some more time. No leniency was forthcoming. The man who had been shown mercy would not extend mercy to someone else. Instead, he unceremoniously threw the man in prison. When the king found out about this, he was outraged. He summoned his servant. "I was willing to forgive you. Could you not found it in your heart to forgive someone else?" (story told in Matthew 18:23-33) Then I realize and acknowledge that I, also a recipient of God's constant and continual forgiveness, have often found myself refusing to forgive someone else.

Recall the heroic death of Stephen, a Hellenistic Jewish Christian who became the first martyr to his newfound faith. The members of the Sanhedrin, a sort of religious Supreme Court, listened with hostility to Stephen's diatribe against them. He was attacking them verbally for replacing a religion of the heart with a religion of man-made rules. He was accusing them of arrogance and self-righteousness. They were not exactly an appreciative audience. (story told in Acts 7)

> When they heard this, they were furious… But Stephen, full of the Holy Spirit, looked up to heaven and saw the glory of God, and Jesus standing at the right hand of God. "Look," he said, "I see heaven open and the Son of Man standing at the right hand of God." At this they covered their ears and, yelling at the top of their voices, they all rushed at him, dragged him out of the city and began to stone him. Meanwhile, the witnesses laid their clothes at the feet of a young man named Saul. While they were stoning him, Stephen prayed, "Lord Jesus, receive my spirit." Then he fell on his knees and cried out, "Lord, do not hold this sin against them." When he had said this, he fell asleep. And Saul was there, giving approval to his death. (Acts 7:54-8:1 NIV)

In his book *From Saul to Paul*, Roy L. Smith said that there were a variety of ways to execute someone but that stoning was among the most gruesome.[1] Standing only about one or two yards away from their victim, the executioners threw their rocks at their helpless target. The damage was frightening: spattered blood, battered flesh, shattered bones. Ultimately the body, ripped to shreds, was unrecognizable.

Yet Stephen faithfully faced this outrage with luminous courage and died with a prayer of forgiveness on his lips. Saul of Tarsus, standing there, consenting to his death, probably would never get that prayer out of his mind.[2] Many biblical commentators have speculated that the church owes St. Paul to the prayer of St. Stephen. Like Stephen, our own prayer of forgiveness can have more impact on someone than stones hurled against flesh.

The personal story of Corrie ten Boom is a soul-stirring drama. She and her Dutch family courageously laid their lives on the line when German troops invaded Holland in World War II. Corrie's family created a hiding place in their home where their Jewish neighbors could hide from the Gestapo. Inadvertently Corrie became a member of the Dutch Underground. Eventually someone betrayed the family, who were subsequently arrested and transported to German concentration camps. Some of them died there.

Corrie survived, and two years after the war ended, she was the guest speaker in several speaking engagements across the war-wrecked European continent. She came to Munich, Germany, where she spoke about the Lord's marvelous forgiveness.

As she concluded her talk, she noticed, out of the corner of her eye, someone walking toward her, deliberately walking against the exiting crowd. As he continued to approach her, she saw him in his hat and trench coat. Then in a sudden flashback, she saw this same middle-aged man dressed in his SS uniform with the dreaded death's head insignia on the visor of his cap. This approaching figure was now a sanitized version of the man he had once been: a Nazi guard at Ravensbruck Concentration Camp. Now her mind went back to that nightmare: the gigantic room, the intense lighting, the piles of women's clothes on the floor, and the humiliation of being forced to parade naked in front of leering guards, especially this man, one of the cruelest guards of all.

Now back here in Munich, he had the audacity to come up to her. She could not handle it. He stood brazenly in front of her and extended his hand in friendship, anxious to shake her own hand. He wanted to congratulate her on making crystal-clear the magnanimity of God's unconditional love. He was filled with enthusiasm as he verbally reviewed the scriptures she had quoted.

In the depths of her soul Corrie shriveled, repulsed by her memory of him. She could not bring herself to shake his extended hand. Never. Ingenuously he told her that once he had been a guard in the very camp where she and her sister had been incarcerated. Since that time, he had become a deeply committed Christian. He knew, deep in his heart, that the Lord had forgiven him, but his question was, could she?[3]

Nailed to the floor, she just stood there, deeply conflicted. She was certainly well-aware that the Lord had forgiven her innumerable times in her own life. She also knew that the Lord had plainly stated, in the Sermon on the Mount, that if we refuse to forgive others, then we cannot expect him to forgive us. She further realized that our unwillingness to forgive will keep us from moving forward. Those who refuse adamantly to forgive are forever locked in the past. On top of all that practical wisdom, she knew that forgiveness is much more than just an emotion; it is a willful act. In short, one must make the decision to forgive despite one's feelings. It was really time for Corrie ten Boom to "put up or shut up."

She earnestly prayed that the Lord would enable her to forgive this man. As she was praying, she offered her hand to the former SS guard. Instantly, at that precise moment, something supernatural occurred. It was as if an electric current passed right through her body, unleashing her tears and setting her free. This unlikely couple stood together for a long moment. Corrie knew that she had made herself a channel for God's redemptive love.[4] "The seen and the unseen"— that creative spark of the Creator God that arcs between our self and another soul whenever we stretch out our hand in forgiveness!

Chapter 16

PRAISE!

Praise—it requires a conscious effort to praise the Lord. After nearly half a century as a pastor, I have observed that people are more concerned about the *style* of their worship than they are about the *attitudes* they bring to worship. So we have wound up with raging arguments over gospel songs and praise choruses versus hymns, over the efficacy of singing out of a hymnal or off a large screen, over the choice of a pipe organ versus an electronic organ versus a keyboard versus guitars and drums. There are definite battle lines drawn between traditional worship and contemporary worship. It can get very confusing. So how are we supposed to praise the Lord?

First, praise should be *thankful*. St. Paul wrote, "Rejoice evermore. Pray without ceasing: In everything give *thanks*: for this is the will of God in Christ Jesus concerning you" (1 Thess. 5:16–18, KJV; emphasis mine) In reflecting upon our act of worship, we can say that God wants us to praise him, not because it is so good for *him* but because it is so good for *us*. It is like teaching a child to say "thank you." Praise does not change God; it changes *us*. Our expression of gratitude dissipates our negative thoughts and feelings like mist before the morning sun. "In everything give *thanks*."

A preacher once shared with Catherine Marshall a riveting story about his friend whose little daughter had succumbed to her sickness. Her father was distraught and embittered by the cruel fact that the Lord had not heeded his impassioned prayers. He took a walk, and standing beneath the night sky, he recognized the fact that his options were limited. As far as he could see, he either could go on waging his private war against God for his betrayal—permitting his little girl to die—or do what the apostle Paul suggested, "In everything give thanks." He knew full well that his heart really was not in his second choice and that his prayers of thanksgiving would be forced and sound contrived. Still, it would be better than his first choice: to rant and rail against one's Creator and further isolate oneself. He thus began to pray. Gathering himself together, he said, "Lord, thank you lending us this beautiful child who blessed our life for two years." From that very moment, he began to heal.[1]

Thanksgiving is a conscious choice that you make: to *give* thanks! Sometimes our circumstances are so terrible that it seems like an impossible choice, yet it is this deliberate choice that ultimately will offer you the greatest reward.

Secondly, our praise should be *joyful*. Regardless of how you label your style of worship, your attitude should be one of joy. Psalm 100 begins, "Make a *joyful* noise unto the Lord, all ye lands. Serve the Lord with gladness: come before his presence with singing" (Ps. 100:1, KJV; emphasis mine)

I vividly recall the time when a young Pentecostal woman, Lee Zengeler, invited me to her church's midweek worship service. It was crowded with young people. Everyone was filled with joy, raising their arms in worship and praise. I felt a bit left out, as if I had come to a wedding reception in my pajamas. I turned to my hostess and said, "Lee, please don't misunderstand me. I don't want to be critical. I'm happy that everyone else is happy, and I wouldn't take it away from them for anything in the world. But personally, I don't happen to *feel* that way. I'm not *feeling* all that joy!"

She listened carefully, then said, "Jerry, do you imagine that all these people came here tonight *feeling* joyful? Don't you imagine that many of them face domestic circumstances that are dark, dismal, and dreary? You are assuming that their exuberant praise emerges out of their joy, that first comes the joy and then the act of praise. In fact, it's just the opposite. First, we *choose* to praise the Lord. As a result of that conscious choice, we experience joy."

In 2 Samuel 6, a curious event occurs. King David's troops were escorting the Ark of the Covenant for the first time, into the city of Jerusalem. This ark symbolized the power and presence of Yahweh, the Lord God.

> David...danced before the Lord with all his might, while he and the entire house of Israel brought up the ark of the Lord with shouts and the sound of trumpets. As the ark of the Lord was entering the city...[David's wife] watched from a window. And when she saw King David leaping and dancing before the Lord, she despised him in her heart. (2 Sam. 6:14–16)

She could not enter into his joy because hers was a "windowsill faith." She wasn't a participant, just an observer. If you find that you are not entering into the joy of worship, it just might be that you are not worshiping from the heart but from the windowsill! And remember Eutychus? It is written in the book of Acts, "Seated in a window was a young man named Eutychus, who was sinking into a deep sleep as Paul talked on and on. When he was sound asleep, he fell to the ground from the third story and was picked up dead" (Acts 20:9). Watch out for windowsills.

Thirdly, our praise should be *free of bitterness*! Look at Leah, for example. In the Old Testament book of Genesis, we learn about her. She was Rachel's sister. She was at best homely; she was just a plain Jane.

> Now Laban had two daughters; the name of the older was Leah, and the name of the younger was Rachel. Leah had weak eyes, but Rachel was lovely in form, and beautiful. (Gen. 29:16–17)

Leah's "weak eyes" was not a description of how she saw but of how she looked. Her eyes probably lacked that sparkle that mesmerizes male admirers. Anyway, Jacob was attracted to the svelte and effervescent Rachel and entered into an agreement with her father that he would work seven years for her hand in marriage. He knew she was worth it.

Then came the big wedding and the appearance of a heavily veiled bride. In one of the first recorded cases of bait and switch, the crafty father-in-law substituted the older and less attractive sister. Jacob wound up with Leah, the plain Jane. Eventually, Jacob also was awarded Rachel, in return for a mere seven years of additional work (Gen. 29:19–27)!

Leah knew in her heart that Jacob did not really love her, but she dutifully bore him three sons, each time hoping that it would make her husband love her (Gen. 29:32–34). Jacob never did. After her first three sons were born, "she conceived again, and when she gave birth to a son she said, 'This time I will praise the Lord.' So she named him Judah, a name that might mean "Praise the Lord". Then she stopped having children" (Gen. 29:35). She deliberately divested herself of her bitterness for having to play second fiddle to her pretty sister. Instead, she chose to praise God. With a grateful heart, she raised Judah. And when Jacob was dying, he assembled his sons for a final blessing. Ironically, the greatest blessing of all was given to Judah. Jacob said, "The scepter will not depart from Judah, nor the ruler's staff from between his feet, until he comes to whom it belongs" (Gen. 49:10a). Leah had seen her rejection by Jacob clearly; she had *not* seen her acceptance by God. For one day, from Leah, not Rachel, the Messiah would come.

Our praise should be thankful, joyful, free of bitterness, and *heartfelt*. Once an angel offered someone a guided tour through a church where the congregation had gathered for worship. The angel escorted him from one area to another. The sanctuary was packed with congregants. However, the visitor soon began to sense a certain strangeness about this place. For instance, the organist's hands moved up and down the keyboard of his instrument without emitting any notes. Choir members opened their mouths and shaped their notes without producing an anthem. The preacher read the Scripture wordlessly. Then he preached without making a sound. The onlooker, hearing nothing at all, was perplexed and asked the angel what this meant.

The angel answered, "You are hearing what God hears. The Lord hears only heartfelt prayer." Just then they heard, from the back of the church, a little prayer uttered by a child. The angel quickly added, "God hears her prayer because she means what she says. He hears the language of the heart."[2] The language of the heart! May the God you cannot always see, always see you. May the God you cannot hear, always *hear* you.

Chapter 17

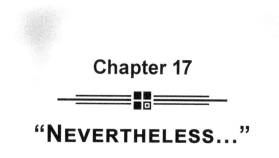

"Nevertheless..."

One day Jesus stood beside the lake while people crowded around him to hear God's Word. I am guessing that he recognized the fact that the suffocating press of the multitude would muffle his voice. He glanced around and spotted two fishing boats that were tied up. Their owners already had been out on the water all night and were just now washing and mending nets. Jesus climbed into one of the boats and beckoned its owner (Simon Peter) to row him out on the lake, a few yards offshore. Then he sat in the boat and taught the people from this floating pulpit (Luke 5:1–3). The backdrop of mountains across the lake perhaps turned this setting into a natural amphitheater in which Jesus's voice could be amplified.

Afterward, as a reward to his volunteer, Jesus offered him a hot tip: "Launch out into the deep, and let down your nets" (Luke 5:4a). Simon Peter probably felt nonplussed by Jesus's effort to be helpful. "Master, we've worked hard all night and haven't caught anything" (Luke 5:5a).

The advice Jesus had given was patently absurd. You fished at night because that's when the fish were feeding, not during the day. The fish weren't biting, and neither was Peter. Probably any fisherman seen fishing in broad daylight automatically would become a laughingstock. Furthermore, no matter how charismatic Jesus might be, he was still an itinerant rabbi who knew nothing about fishing. Simon Peter was the commercial fisherman, the expert.

Yet there was something so authoritative in Jesus's voice and commanding about His presence that Peter answered, "Master, we have toiled all the night, and have taken nothing: *nevertheless* at thy word I will let down the net" (Luke 5:5, KJV; emphasis mine). What an illustration of trustful obedience! Simon Peter was saying, "In spite of all the evidence to the contrary, in spite of the seeming absurdity of your suggestion, in spite of my personal knowledge of fish, in spite of my own 'street smarts,' I will *nevertheless* do as you say. I will let down my net."

Like Simon Peter, you may have heard the crystal-clear voice of Christ sounding and resounding in your heart and mind, instructing you to respond in a certain way. But perhaps because the instructions made no sense to you at that moment, or perhaps seemed contrary to your own self-interest and natural inclinations, you tuned out his voice. That's my story! I've often heard his voice, not in words but in a supernatural compulsion, and scrambled to make excuses for not heeding his direction. "Master, I already fished there and came up empty-handed. Don't ask me to go back. It doesn't make sense"— when we respond like that, God doesn't then chase us around with lightning bolts; we just miss the blessing we might have had.

There are lots of instances in Scripture where Jesus's counsel has not made sense to me. For one, in the Sermon on the Mount, Jesus said, "For if you forgive men when they sin against you, your heavenly Father will also forgive you. But if you do not forgive men their sins, your Father will not forgive your sins" (Matt. 6:14–15). Maybe I feel like I cannot forgive someone else because the hurt goes too deep. Does he really expect me to do what seems so impossible to me?

So many times I have felt his nudging. In Isaiah it is written: "Whether you turn to the right or to the left, your ears will hear a voice behind you, saying, 'This is the way; walk in it'" (Isa. 30:21). So many times I have heard his voice and offered my sincerest apologies for not heeding what he says. Each of us finally needs to say, "Lord, this guidance of yours doesn't make any sense to me. *Nevertheless*, at thy word, I will do what you say! I will let down my net!" John Greenleaf Whittier wrote:

> In simple trust like theirs who heard,
> Beside the Syrian Sea,
> The gracious calling of the Lord,
> Let us, like them, without a word,
> Rise up and follow Thee.[1]

That single word, *nevertheless*, is precious. In Gethsemane, the Lord's destiny—and ours—hinged upon these words: "Father, if thou be willing, remove this cup from me; *nevertheless* not my will, but thine, be done" (Luke 22:42, KJV; emphasis mine). Calamities come our way, "*nevertheless* I am not ashamed: for I know whom I have believed" (2 Tim. 1:12b, KJV; emphasis mine).

Marion Bond West poignantly described her husband's battle with a life-threatening affliction. He faced critical surgery for a brain tumor. All her life, Marion had been tormented by the what-ifs that emerge in the shadow of our thinking. What if her husband's employment vanished, or a child was injured in an accident, or her husband's brain tumor proved to be malignant? What if he didn't make it? Her worst fears were realized when the surgeons informed her that the tumor indeed was malignant and that her husband had only a few months.[2]

Then as a godsend, there came into her mind one simple word: *nevertheless*! Instantly she recognized that the Lord was with her. Even if her husband were to succumb, as the doctors expected, he would find healing in a larger world beyond this one.[3] As she studied her Bible, she saw this word repeated over ninety times. One example of this is the scripture in Galatians, "I am crucified with Christ: *nevertheless* I live" (Gal. 2:20a, KJV; emphasis mine).

Very early on a Sunday morning, her husband passed away. "*Nevertheless*" assured the Lord's closeness, and she was able to go on, sustained by a single word.[4]

In the profound seventy-third Psalm, the psalmist struggled with all the injustices he saw around him. From his perspective, it was clear that wicked people prospered while the innocent suffered. The absence of divine intervention perplexed him. Finally, he saw everything through new lenses; he saw the unseen and went on to write this mighty affirmation of faith:

> *Nevertheless* I am continually with thee: thou hast holden me by my right hand. Thou shalt guide me with thy counsel, and afterward receive me to glory. Whom have I in heaven but thee? And there is none upon earth that I desire beside thee. My flesh and my heart faileth: but God is the strength of my heart, and my portion forever. (Ps. 73:23–26, KJV; emphasis mine)

Into your life will come conflicts that threaten to overwhelm your mind and crush your spirit; *nevertheless,* "he who promised is faithful" (Heb. 10:23b).

Chapter 18

FAILURE

Do you ever feel paralyzed by your fear of failure? Nobody wants to fail. Nobody likes feeling defeated. Nobody wants to feel like a loser. In fact, most people would prefer not to try at all than to try and subsequently fail. It is easier not to try. In a book entitled *Transformed By Thorns*, there is a story of a young boy who was totally frustrated by the performance of his baseball team. They had managed to lose almost every game they had played that season. And he was as bad as the rest of his team. Then one day the boy complained about this to his sister, who, in an effort to encourage him, said, "Timmy, don't you realize that you learn more from your failures than from your success?"

Timmy responded, "If that's true, then I'm one of the world's smartest baseball players."[1] I have a hunch that Timmy would much rather be a stupid winner than a smart loser.

All of us try to rationalize our personal failures, but none of us appreciates the exercise. We each crave success. But what constitutes success? *My first observation* is that, in the Lord's eyes, what we call success might really be failure and what we see as failure might be success.

In a book of devotions, Dan Weaver noted that we all would like to be a success—like Simon Peter, who preached a winning sermon to a multitude on the day of Pentecost. However, Stephen preached an identical sermon and got stoned to death. To our knowledge there was only one person in Stephen's audience who became a Christian[2]—only one person: his name, the apostle Paul.

One day our eleven-year-old granddaughter, Danielle, was a participant in a modeling contest. As grandparents, my wife and I felt duty-bound to attend and wave flags and pom-poms for her. We watched about 172 attractive young women compete in four separate categories: preteen, junior teen, teen, and Ms. Philadelphia. During the course of competition, each candidate had to model a casual outfit, model a formal outfit, and finally, answer this single mind-stretching question: "How would you define a winner?"

All the contestants offered virtually the same answer. Some answered with poise and composure; others, with somewhat less stage presence. Still, each wound up stating that a winner is someone who sets a goal for herself and then achieves it.

Later, as our family was eating together at a restaurant, our son (Danielle's father) commented on those answers. He said, "How else could you possibly define the word *winner*? Obviously, a winner is someone who sets a goal and then achieves it. What other answer could you possibly give!"

I looked at my son with barely suppressed amusement and said, "Paul, that's the *wrong* answer. All the contestants got it wrong. Adolf Hitler set a goal for himself in the infamous Final Solution: the extermination of Europe's Jews. He largely achieved his goal, eliminating six million. So does that, by definition, make him a winner? No, to be a winner means more than just achieving your goal. It means choosing the *right* goal. If you do that, you still can be a winner, even if you fail. The Lord isn't calling you to be successful in the *world's* eyes but in *His*."

My second observation is that the Lord is the Master of bringing success out of failure. In his book *Hope for the Troubled Heart*, Billy Graham retold the story of a man who survived the sinking of his ship. He made it to a deserted island, where he eventually constructed a shelter for himself. There he stored everything he had managed to salvage from the shipwreck. Night and day, he prayed to be rescued and desperately searched the sea for a passing ship. Then a day came when his little hut caught fire, and everything he owned was incinerated in the resulting conflagration: an unmitigated catastrophe! Within a short time, a ship arrived to rescue him. "We saw your flare," the captain said. Out of what seemed to be a tragedy had come a blessing.[3]

Scripture says, "And we know that in all things God works for the good of those who love him, who have been called according to his purpose" (Rom. 8:28). Billy Graham observed that if you were carefully to taste the individual ingredients for a cake, none of them would be very appetizing: flour, raw eggs, baking powder! But if you mix them all together, you can obtain a scrumptious result. In just the same way, the Lord can take your struggles and transform them into a good outcome.[4] He can transform your failure into success—"the seen and the unseen" (2 Cor. 4:18)!

My own most miserable experience of dismal failure occurred in a little church in Bucks County, Pennsylvania. The blue-collar town in which I pastored was said to have three churches and twenty-six bars. Furthermore, this was the early 1970s, and we were awash with drugs. People were celebrating their unbridled freedom to do anything they wanted, resulting not in the anticipated delight but in unexpected despair. The whole town needed somehow to be reconnected with God.

Then I inadvertently discovered a possible vehicle for evangelism (in fact, several vehicles!). The Christian Wheels Motorcycle Club, headquartered in a neighboring town, was a committed band of Protestant Pentecostal and Catholic Charismatics, men and women who were unembarrassed witnesses for Christ. I considered inviting them to come to our church one Saturday night a month and minister to the whole community. My agenda was not to use this plan to enlarge my own church but to enlarge the kingdom of God. We envisioned audiences comprised of kids off the street: stealers, dealers, drug addicts—whoever was there.

Excited, the members of the club immediately accepted the invitation, but our church board was reticent. They needed to examine this from every angle because there were several considerations:

insurance risks, property risks, etc. Maybe drug dealers would steal our public address system. I readily acknowledged that their concerns were legitimate but added that transformed lives were worth the risk. The church's property should not determine its programs; the tail shouldn't wag the dog. The Christian lifestyle and mind-set mandated that we should be willing to engage in risk-taking in order to achieve God's larger purposes. The church board agreed.

Thus, The Christian Wheels Motorcycle Club *came*. The townspeople *came*. Those on the margins of society—the stealers, the dealers, and the drug addicts—*came*. And our public address system *went*. Our worst fears were realized. The board members had warned me this would happen. I had exposed my own church to exploitation. I felt used. All I could see was my personal failure as a pastor. What I could not see were all the people that were healed, the souls that were saved, and the hearts that were filled with the Holy Spirit as a result of our outreach. By God's grace, it was not a failure after all.

Take another look at Jesus's followers. Once Simon Peter had said to his Lord, "We have left everything to follow you" (Mark 10:28). It was literally true. They had sacrificed their homes, families, friends, and livelihoods to follow him. Then came the unthinkable, the unbearable: the crucifixion. The meaning and purpose of their life evaporated. Not only had Jesus's ministry ended in failure, but so had theirs. They imagined that they were hitching their wagon to a star, but that turned out to be a falling star.

Then one morning, two of Jesus's followers were walking to the village of Emmaus, feeling down and defeated. A Stranger, out of the blue, appeared beside them. They didn't recognize him. He brazenly intruded upon the privacy of their grief. They fell into whispering to one another.

"What are you two talking about?" he asked.

Reluctantly, they told him the story of Jesus and then added, "We had so hoped that he was the Messiah." Then the Stranger reminded them of biblical prophecies concerning the Messiah.

When they reached the village, the men invited the Stranger to stay with them (Luke 24:13–29). During dinner, in an old familiar gesture, "he took bread, gave thanks, broke it and began to give it to them. Then their eyes were opened and they recognized *Him*, and he disappeared from their sight" (Luke 24:30b–31; emphasis mine) By God's grace, it wasn't a failure after all. Jesus was alive, in a brand-new way. And they had radiant light for their journey ahead.

Chapter 19

INTERRUPTIONS: TIME OUT FOR GOD

Have you ever noticed that on certain occasions, time rushes by like an unstoppable raging stream, and on other occasions, it creeps like sludge? For instance, when I was ten years old, in fifth grade, I was ordered to the principal's office. I almost suffered a nervous breakdown as I walked down the hall in fear and trembling. Then I had to sit on a bench outside his office while I waited to be summoned. In the principal's perception of time, as he sat ensconced behind his massive desk, only five minutes had passed by before he commanded my presence. For me, it seemed like two weeks. There certainly are those times when time *trickles*.

Other times, it *zooms*. My wife might casually ask, "Do you remember Sally Ann Nuss?"

"Of course! She was my next-door neighbor, a kid about seven years old."

"Well," says my wife, "her granddaughter just had a baby."

"Her granddaughter? Sally Ann is only seven!" Can time really go by that fast?

Most of us are aware of the time warp between Christmases. When you are a child, there are eighteen months between Christmases. When you are a "senior citizen," there are only four! So there are occasions when time trickles and other occasions when it zooms.

Then there are moments, precious moments, when time *stands still*—scintillating, shining, sparkling, and shimmering. It could be a celestial, supernatural moment when God's eternity breaks into human time. Whenever that "breakthrough" occurs, we must take *time out for God*. Live the moment. There is a hymn in which we sing these words:

> Take time to be holy, speak oft with thy Lord;
> Abide in him always, and feed on his word...
> Take time to be holy, the world rushes on...[1]

Now we come to the story of Mary and Martha, a story guaranteed to irritate housewives everywhere. These two sisters lived with their brother, Lazarus, in the little village of Bethany, just two miles outside Jerusalem. "As Jesus and his disciples were on their way, he came to a village where a woman named Martha opened her home to him. She had a sister called Mary, who sat at the Lord's feet listening to what he said. But Martha was distracted by all the preparations that had to be made. She came to him and asked, 'Lord, don't you care that my sister has left me to do the work by myself? Tell her to help me!' 'Martha, Martha,' the Lord answered, 'you are worried and upset about many things, but only one thing is needed: Mary has chosen what is better, and it will not be taken away from her'" (Luke 10:38–42).

Take a hard look at this picture. Here are two sisters, presumably enjoying the privacy of their own home, when Jesus drops in on them. He's also brought twelve friends! What an interruption to domestic tranquility! Food has to be miraculously produced (and Jesus might be better at this than Martha!). Martha panics. She makes a beeline for the kitchen while her sister just sits dreamily at Jesus's feet. Every time Martha peeps around the corner, she feels annoyed with Mary.

Reflecting on the scene, I figure that I am by nature more of a Mary than a Martha—not because I am so spiritual but because I am so lazy! Sometimes my wife berates me, "You just sit there! Look at you just sitting! You don't see all that needs to be done around here! You never even look! You could live in a pile of dirt and be happy!"

It is true. I would rather sit and listen to someone than slave over a hot stove.

I feel bad for Martha, who was, as they say, working her fingers to the bone. And on top of that, adding insult to injury, Jesus complimented the *other* sister! "Mary has chosen what is better," he said (Luke 10:42). In his Sermon on the Mount, Jesus had said, "But seek ye first the kingdom of God" (Matthew 6:33a KJV). What was just an interruption for Martha was a holy moment for Mary, when she sat still, when time stood still, when she discovered herself in the presence of God.

When I was pastoring a small church in the Olney neighborhood of Philadelphia, I received a 2:00 a.m. phone call. Here was an interruption if I ever heard one. Richard Leaver, a young man in my congregation, wanted to see me right away. I was so tempted to tell him to take two aspirin and call me in the morning, yet I also believed that I should address a crisis at the moment the crisis presented itself. Some so-called interruptions are really holy moments that come to us, quite literally, as godsends. Whenever one such moment comes, take *time out for God*.

When Richard entered, he immediately requested prayer. He actually knelt on the living room floor, inviting me to kneel beside him, and committed himself to serving the Lord as a pastor. He ultimately became a pastor with a wonderful healing ministry.

In our Lord's own ministry, interruptions sporadically occurred. Each became an opportunity to respond to human need.

One day a Canaanite woman, a Gentile, approached him and cried for his healing touch on behalf of her afflicted daughter. She intruded on his privacy, but he let time stand still, "and her daughter was healed from that very hour" (Matt. 15:28b) On another day, a group of mothers interrupted Jesus by dragging their children to his side. His disciples were annoyed by this intrusion, but Jesus made time for the children, saying, "Let the little children come to me, and do not hinder them, for the kingdom of heaven belongs to such as these." (Matt. 19:14) Children often make demands upon us, yet as we reach out to them, quite unseen by us, the hand of an invisible God is reaching to caress them.

In the fifth chapter of Mark, there is a curious sequence of events:

> When Jesus had again crossed over by boat to the other side of the lake, a large crowd gathered around him while he was by the lake. Then one of the synagogue rulers, named Jairus, came there. Seeing Jesus, he fell at his feet and pleaded earnestly with him, "My little daughter is dying. Please come and put your hands on her so that she will be healed and live." So Jesus went with him. A large crowd followed and pressed around him. (Mark 5:21–24)

> And a woman was there who had been subject to bleeding for twelve years. She had suffered a great deal under the care of many doctors and had spent all she had, yet instead of getting better she grew worse. When she heard about Jesus, she came up behind him in the crowd and touched his cloak, because she thought, "If I just touch his clothes, I will be healed." Immediately her bleeding stopped and she felt in her body that she was freed from her suffering. (Mark 5:25–29)

Look at what had just transpired! A father named Jairus had interrupted Jesus. Then just as Jesus was in the process of responding to this father's need, along came this afflicted woman who intruded on Jairus's time just as Jesus was en route to help him. So what you wind up with is an interruption and then an interruption of an interruption. I can just see Jairus turning to this second petitioner and saying, "Well excuse me! *I* interrupted him *first*! In case you don't know it, you happen to be interrupting my interruption!" Yet our Lord made time for each of them.

Throughout your own life, you will feel like you are being chased around a large dial by the hands of a clock that move inexorably to sweep over you. Nevertheless, there will be special moments, holy moments, when time stands still. Inevitably, there also will be interruptions that disrupt your journey. Some of them will seem silly or trivial—the seen and the unseen! Not every *inter*ruption is a *dis*ruption of God's plan. Sometimes, completely unseen by you, the interruption *is* God's plan.

Chapter 20

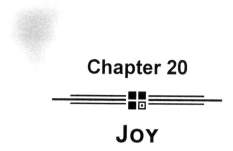

JOY

I told the story earlier of how I vividly remember standing beside a bride at her wedding reception and hearing an exchange between her and a wedding guest. The guest said something like, "I wish you all the luck in the world," to which the bride responded ingenuously, "I just want to be *happy*!" Both statements struck me as silly things to say. First, marriages are not based on luck. Secondly, every person just wants to be happy too. But it's not an entitlement, and there are no guarantees.

Happiness seems to be dependent on outward circumstances; *joy* is dependent on an inward relationship with God. Happiness comes and goes; joy abides. Joy has staying power. Here is a philosophical question for you to consider: is it possible to be unhappy and yet harbor a deep joy? I believe the answer is yes. Your outward circumstances might change adversely, but your relationship with the Lord remains steadfast. The Christian faith does not guarantee you happiness; it guarantees you *joy*. You will discover this joy serendipitously as you put Jesus first.

Once when I attended an annual ministerial conference, we first had to register and then carry our luggage to our assigned rooms. In my room, on the desk, was a packet of prepared material. Inside the packet was a little red button with the white numeral 3. Attached was an explanation. Each seminar participant was requested to wear it on his lapel, signifying his intention to put Jesus first, others second, and him or herself third. I very dutifully put the button on.

At the noontime luncheon, I met fellow participants who had not yet been to their rooms. "What's that red button for?" they asked, pointing to my lapel.

"Oh," I answered proudly, "it means that I'm willing to put Jesus first, others second, and myself third."

"You put yourself third?"

"Of course!"

"Then why do you have to wear the button?"

A perfect squelch! By wearing a little red button proclaiming that I wasn't calling attention to myself, I was paradoxically calling attention to myself. Joy never comes directly but indirectly as we lose ourselves in others and in God.

> A wedding took place at Cana in Galilee. Jesus' mother was there, and Jesus and his disciples had also been invited to the wedding. When the wine was gone, Jesus' mother said to him, "They have no more wine." (John 2:1–3)

William Barclay commented that having wine on the menu at a wedding reception was obligatory. To run out of wine, particularly at a wedding, would be a social faux pas and a huge embarrassment to the family.[1]

> "They have no more wine."
> "Dear woman, why do you involve me?" Jesus replied, "My time has not yet come."
> His mother said to the servants, "Do whatever he tells you." (John 2:3b–5)

Mary knew her Son! She knew that he would respond to people's needs. He was about to perform his first miracle, and he would do it to spare a family from humiliation. He knew what they were going through.²

Now this is what happened:

> Nearby stood six stone water jars, the kind used by the Jews for ceremonial washing, each holding from twenty to thirty gallons. Jesus said to the servants, "Fill the jars with water"; so they filled them to the brim. Then he told them, "Now draw some out and take it to the master of the banquet." (John 2:6–8a)

What? The servants must have wondered what the Master of Ceremonies was going to do with a hundred and fifty gallons of *water*!

Sometimes, with all our attention to the details, we manage to miss seeing the miracle. We simply are oblivious to its appearance. Hasn't it happened that way in your own life?

> The master of the banquet tasted the water that had been turned into wine. He did not realize where it had come from, though the servants who had drawn the water knew. Then he called the bridegroom aside and said, "Everyone brings out the choice wine first and then the cheaper wine after the guests have had too much to drink; [and by this time can't tell the difference] but you have saved the best till now." (John 2:9–10)

Once when I was in Jerusalem, I heard the Anglican priest at Christ Church Hospice say, "When Jesus gives, he gives in abundance. And he gives the very best!"

> This, the first of his miraculous signs, Jesus performed in Cana of Galilee. He thus revealed his glory, and his disciples put their faith in him. (John 2:11)

Jesus had turned water into wine. He had brought them joy. (Incidentally, we United Methodists usually tell this story the other way around: Jesus turns all the wine into water.) He added the sparkle; he made the fizz. What does that mean for your life? Whenever *you* run out of juice, whenever you are spiritually exhausted or all used up, whenever your life goes flat, he is here to turn the water into wine. Once Jesus said, "These things have I spoken unto you, that my joy might remain in you, and that your joy might be full" (John 15:11, KJV).

We see with only our senses. Like the servants and the Master of Ceremonies, we see the water but miss the wine. We see the reds, yellows, and blues of life, but we miss the infrareds and the ultraviolets. We see our problems, but we miss his presence. We need a spiritual extrasensory perception that sees *him*. Long ago the psalmist wrote, "In thy presence is fullness of joy" (Ps. 16:11, KJV).

A renowned Bible scholar, Dr. R. A. Torrey, was devastated when he and his wife lost their twelve-year-old daughter, who died in a tragic accident. On a rainy day, they stood forlornly beside the grave as her body was laid to rest. Dr. Torrey's wife expressed her consolation that their daughter was not really in that casket—only her body—and that their little girl, Elizabeth, was in the presence of the Lord. Still, their hearts were broken. Her absence from their lives would create a terrible emptiness.

One day, while he was walking along, that awful sense of loss hit Dr. Torrey with full force. He didn't know how to deal with it. There was nowhere else to go but to the Lord. In that moment of prayer, he felt drenched by a downpour of God's love. Joy bubbled up within him, for he knew that God would be with them through it all.[3] Jesus said, "Before long, the world will not see me anymore, but you will see me (John 14:19a)…I will see you again and you will rejoice, and no one will take away your *joy*" (John 16:22b; emphasis mine).

Chapter 21

WORRY

In his Sermon on the Mount, Jesus shared with all of us a total way of life that focuses not only on our actions and their resulting consequences but also on our underlying motives and attitudes.

> Therefore I tell you, do not *worry* about your life, what you will eat or drink; or about your body, what you will wear...Look at the birds of the air; they do not sow or reap or store away in barns, and yet your heavenly Father feeds them. Are you not much more valuable than they? Who of you by *worrying* can add a single hour to his life? (Matt. 6:25a, 26–27; emphasis mine)

> Therefore do not *worry* about tomorrow...Each day has enough trouble of its own. (Matt. 6:34a, c; emphasis mine).

Worries! We worry about *having* them. And we worry about *not* having them. Someone once told me that if they suddenly discovered that they had nothing to worry about, they'd worry about having nothing to worry about. And somewhere I read about a psychiatric patient who sat in his hospital room, pressing his ear against the wall.

Curious, a staff member walked over to investigate. The patient saw her approaching and whispered to her to be very quiet. The hospital worker tiptoed up to the wall, pressed her ear against it, and listened intently for several minutes. Finally she concluded, "I don't hear anything."

"Neither do I," said the patient. "It's been like that all day!"

We *worry* not only about what's happening but also about what *could* or *might* happen. Is this true of you? Then you might as well pull up a wall!

A woman in my church once told me about the time she retrieved her second grader from school. Her son seemed unusually solemn as he climbed into the car. He sat morosely during the ride home. Finally his mother broke the silence by asking, "Honey, what's wrong?"

"I just had the second worst day of my life!" he declared.

"I'm so sorry," his mom replied. They continued riding in silence. At length his mother commented, "By the way, you said you just had the '*second*' worst' day of your life. What was the worst?"

"I don't know," he answered, "I haven't had it yet!"

There's pessimism for you! He was just waiting for, and *worrying* about, the oncoming catastrophe. I bet that five *minutes* of prayer beats five *hours* of worry, every time!

There's an instructive story related in 2 Chronicles 20. Nine hundred years before Christ, the armies of the Moabites and the Ammonites ganged up against the little nation of Judah. King Jehoshaphat was informed of this new and frightening threat to his country:

> "A vast army is coming against you from…the other side of the [Dead] Sea. It is already [on our side of the Dead Sea]." Alarmed, Jehoshaphat resolved to inquire of the Lord, and he proclaimed a fast for all Judah. The people of Judah came together to seek help from the Lord; indeed, they came from every town in Judah to seek him." (2 Chron. 20:1–4)

Next to the combined armies of this aggressive alliance, Judah's tiny army must have resembled a Cub Scout Pack. In their panic, the people of Judah assembled to seek the Lord. Do you do that yourself when you're confronted by some insurmountable difficulty, some paralyzing crisis? When the odds are stacked against you? Do you seek out God's resources, or do you simply rely on your own? Do you pray, or just worry yourself sick?

> Then Jehoshaphat stood up in the assembly of Judah and Jerusalem at the temple of the Lord…and said: "O Lord, God of our fathers….You rule over the kingdoms of the nations. Power and might are in your hand, and no one can withstand you. O our God, did you not…give [this land] forever to the descendants of Abraham your friend?…But now here are [our enemies]…See how they are…coming to drive us out of [this land] you gave us as an inheritance. O our God, will you not judge them? For we have no power to face this vast army that is attacking us. We do not know what to do, but our eyes are upon you." (2 Chron. 20:5–12)

And there's the antidote to worry. When you don't know where to look, try up.

What we see in the king's prayer is faith in slow-motion. As he focuses on the Lord in the midst of his inner turmoil, he begins to see everything from another perspective. He certainly sees Judah's enemies arrayed against him, a scant fifteen hours march away. He sees the mortal danger. But then he sees something else. Through the prism of prayer, he sees the promises and presence of a caring God. Remember what the writer of the epistle to the Hebrews said of Moses: "He persevered because he *saw* him who is invisible" (Heb. 11:27; emphasis mine). He saw the unseen. My favorite definition of *faith* is the acronym: forsaking all, I trust him.

So what happened to Jehoshaphat?

> Then the Spirit of the Lord came upon Jahaziel...
> as he stood in the assembly. He said: "Listen,
> King Jehoshaphat and all who live in Judah and
> Jerusalem! This is what the Lord says to you:
> 'Do not be afraid or discouraged because of
> this vast army. For the battle is not yours, but
> God's. Tomorrow march down against them.'" (2
> Chron. 20:14–16a)

Hear that? "Tomorrow." Not *today* but *tomorrow*! Don't panic. Don't make any sudden moves. Relax. *Tomorrow*!

Then the Lord said, "You will not have to fight this battle. Take up your positions; stand firm and see the deliverance the Lord will give you...Do not be afraid; do not be discouraged. Go out to face them tomorrow, and the Lord will be with you" (2 Chron. 20:17). As someone once paraphrased, "Don't just *do* something; *stand* there!" Long ago the psalmist had written, "Some trust in chariots and some in horses, but we trust in the name of the Lord our God" (Psalm 20:7).

We see our problems; we fail to see God's presence. Our worries are like enemy soldiers arrayed against us. Indeed, the odds against us are sometimes overwhelming. There was a time in ancient Israel when the Syrians, engaging in border clashes with Israel, made an incursion into its territory. Elisha the prophet warned the King of Israel not to venture into the area of Syrian infiltration. Meantime, the King of Syria was informed that this prophet was a probable spy. "Go out and capture him!" he ordered. So a strong Syrian reconnaissance force quickly was deployed like a noose around Elisha. They surrounded the city where he was staying.

The next morning Elisha's servant happened to spot the enemy army. "What are we going to do?" he asked despairingly.

Elisha told him not to worry. Really? Not to worry? Outflanked, outnumbered, and outgunned? Not to worry?

"No," replied the prophet confidently, "there are more of us than of them" (2 Kings 6:8–16). "And Elisha prayed, 'O Lord, open his eyes so he may see.' Then the Lord opened the servant's eyes, and he looked and saw the hills full of horses and chariots of fire all around Elisha" (2 Kings 6:17)—the seen and the unseen (2 Cor. 4:18)!

We see the enemy but not the angels, the chariots of iron but not the chariots of fire, the presence of the enemy but not the presence of the Lord. The psalmist wrote, "The angel of the Lord encamps around those who fear him, and he delivers them. Taste and see that the Lord is good; blessed is the man who takes refuge in him" (Ps. 34:7–8). There's always more than meets the eye. His power is more than a match for your problems. That's why we cherish these words of assurance: "The Lord is my light and my salvation; whom shall I fear? The Lord is the strength of my life; of whom shall I be afraid?" (Ps. 27:1, KJV).

Chapter 22

REJECTION

One of the worst feelings in the world—for any of us—is the feeling of rejection. Whenever anyone rejects us, it crushes our spirit. Throughout my pastoral ministry, there have been different individuals who have said to me, "I don't know how to take you." When people don't know how to "take" you, they usually don't bother "taking" you at all. It's tantamount to rejection. Your personality is so inscrutable that they're not going to waste their time trying to decipher it. Rejection! We've each experienced it, and it really hurts.

During the 1970s, at a time when sensitivity seminars were all the rage, I attended one where the whole group was instructed to form a tight circle and keep the designated "outsider" out. In a marvelous bit of typecasting, I was selected to be the outsider. Desperately I tried barging in, but each effort was effectively blocked. I laughed affably. However, after a while, it did not feel like a game anymore. All the burning feelings of rejection that I ever had suffered were reignited. Even though I was a grown man, the little child within me was in tears.

There are three lessons I have learned from the experience of rejection. *First*, the Lord understands how you feel because he was rejected too. He eventually was rejected by his own family, his hometown, his synagogue, and his people. Rejection hurts most when it comes from someone you love the most. Remember that St. John wrote in his prologue, "He was in the world, and the world was made by him, and the world knew him not. He came unto his own, and his own received him not" (John 1:10–11, KJV).

Jesus's rejection had been prophesied centuries earlier when Isaiah wrote, "He is despised and rejected of men; a man of sorrows, and acquainted with grief: and we hid as it were our faces from him; he was despised, and we esteemed him not" (Isa. 53:3, KJV). So whenever you personally experience the agony of rejection, remember that Jesus went that way before you. That's why it's written in Hebrews: "For we do not have a high priest who is unable to sympathize with our weaknesses, but we have one who has been tempted in every way, just as we are…yet was without sin. Let us then approach the throne of grace with confidence, so that we may receive mercy and find grace to help us in our time of need" (Heb. 4:15–16).

Secondly, because Jesus understands rejection, he will never reject *you*. Once he said, "And whoever comes to me I will never drive away" (John 6:37b). No matter who else rejects us, there is One who remains steadfast, whose love never will let us go.

In a perceptive book entitled *Habitation of Dragons*, Keith Miller told a heart-rending story. He was part of a share group that was focusing on how to live a committed Christian life. As they shared their stories, one reticent young woman named Alice ventured to relate her own experience of growing up as a foster child. She explained that she did not possess an attractive appearance or personality. She wasn't cute and cuddly. Nobody wanted her. Still she went on longing to be adopted by a loving family who would cherish her.

Then one wonderful day, she was informed that a family was coming to take her home. Parenthetically she also was told that there was a trial period, but in her enthusiasm, Alice dismissed that unacceptable thought. After all, this was her dream come true.

Alice settled down with her new family and enrolled in school. She just was beginning to experience a sense of optimism. The one terrible day she came home from school and walked into an empty house. No one was there to welcome her. Instead, her luggage sat in the middle of the floor. Gradually she understood what this meant. Nobody wanted her—nobody!

Alice paused momentarily in her narrative, but each of her listeners found him or herself standing in that empty hallway, staring at the little suitcase and personally experiencing that emptiness and loneliness. When Alice recovered her composure, she quietly stated that this same scenario was repeated more than half a dozen times before her thirteenth birthday. Aware of how deeply moved her audience was, she told them not to pity her because it was precisely those events that led her to the Lord,[1] to a Lord who never will reject us!

Our daughter Jean, an elementary school teacher in the city of Philadelphia, related a similar story. In her first grade class she had a student named Lenice, who was perpetually a loner, standing apart from the other kids. Jean was concerned about her constantly. Then one day Lenice approached our daughter and poured out her heart. "Mrs. Gabl, I've always lived in foster homes. They keep getting rid of me. It's happening again, and I don't know why. I have to go away from my house and my school, and I know I'll never see you again. That's why I never bother making any friends—because I know I'll never see them again when my foster parents send me away!" She sobbed and clung to her teacher.

Even though Jean, as a public school teacher, was supposed to assiduously resist sharing her personal faith with her students, she found this moment, this crisis, irresistible. Hugging her tightly, Jean said, "Remember, Lenice, that Jesus will always be there for you wherever you go and will never stop loving you." Then she pressed into her hand a little wooden heart that said, "Jesus Loves You." Ultimately, it was a gift from *Jesus* to this little girl. Even if everyone in the world rejects you, the Lord never will "for he hath said, I will never leave thee, nor forsake thee" (Heb. 13:5b, KJV).

The third lesson from rejection is this: we must never reject anyone else. Since each of us is well aware of how bad it feels, since each of us is familiar with its many destructive repercussions, we should never inflict that on anyone. We don't clearly see that in rejecting anyone, we are rejecting Christ.

In one church I pastored, when I was very young, I never could find acceptance. I happened to be following two very distinguished predecessors and was a shadow of their former selves. Constantly, I was being compared unfavorably with them. The harder I tried to be accepted, the greater the futility. Then the Lord spoke to my heart. He put this thought into my mind: "Listen. I sent you here to love these people. Your job is not to *be* accepted but to *accept*. Your task is not to *be* loved but to *love*. Stop focusing on yourself. Focus instead on them."

In his profound prayer, St. Francis of Assisi prayed:

> Lord, make me an instrument of Thy peace;
> Where there is hatred, let me sow love;
> Where there is injury, pardon;
> Where there is doubt, faith;
> Where there is despair, hope;
> Where there is darkness, light;
> Where there is sadness, joy.
> O Divine Master,
> Grant that I may not so much seek
> To be consoled, as to console;
> To be understood, as to understand;
> To be loved, as to love.
> For it is in giving that we receive;
> It is in pardoning that we are pardoned;
> And it is in dying that we are born
> To eternal life.
> Amen.[2]

Chapter 23

THE SHATTERED DREAM

Each of us has a dream that we cherish. I recall a day, long ago, when my son's fiancée described to me her dream for her future. She was twenty years old, and her head was spinning around like a globe. She had so many elaborate plans for her life: a little cottage tucked away in the countryside, a floral garden, the obligatory white picket fence, an adjoining garage cradling a classic car, a formal in-the-ground pool, a high-achieving husband, and vacations around the world. As she continued to rhapsodize about her highest hopes and dreams, I could not see my son fitting into them. After a while, neither could she!

Yet each of us persists in entertaining these dreams, which perhaps function to soften the jagged edges of our realities. However, those moments come when our most precious dreams are shattered. How then do we react in the face of disappointment? Often we become disillusioned with God. Isn't he supposed to be in charge?

Recall this promise in the thirty-seventh psalm: "Delight thyself in the Lord; and he shall give thee the desires of thine heart. Commit thy way unto the Lord; trust also in him; and he shall bring it to pass" (Ps. 37:4–5, KJV). But when he doesn't, when the dream fails to materialize, we instantly are deflated. We invested everything we had, we banked all our hopes on him, we went for broke, and we lost our whole investment! It is possible that we misunderstood the promise. When the Bible says, "Delight thyself in the Lord; and he shall give thee the desires of thine heart," (Ps. 37:4, KJV), that doesn't simply mean that the Lord has consented to become your personal vending machine. It simply and profoundly means that if you genuinely delight in the Lord, you will delight in *his* will for your life. Then what *you* want for yourself and what *God* already wants for you will be the same!

I recently spent some time thinking back over my own life: the dreams I nurtured, the choices I made. I was raised in a little Methodist church, regularly attending Sunday school and youth fellowship. Yet I was only a nominal Christian. By the end of college, I felt compelled to attend seminary so that I could examine the Christian faith in depth, explore its beliefs, stand in front of a full-length mirror, and try them on. I intended to explore this faith objectively! My dream was to attend Union Theological Seminary in New York City. It had assembled a faculty of distinguished professors. I therefore applied to Union, and just in case I was not accepted, I also applied to Harvard Divinity School in Cambridge, a seminary I considered just a backup.

In response to my applications, I received a letter from Union—my first choice—requesting that I come up and be interviewed by some representatives of their admissions committee. As I read and reread the letter, I was perplexed. Did the seminary request that *every* applicant make a personal appearance? When I asked our college chaplain why he thought I was sent such a letter, he immediately answered, "Because you're a borderline case!" That observation somewhat hurt my feelings, but I imagined his guess was correct, swallowed my pride, and traveled to New York City.

Three different professors interviewed me separately. One remarked candidly, "It seems to me, from your application, that you could just as easily become a social worker. I mean, you want to help others, but you've expressed no genuine commitment to Christ." I did not want to be dishonest with him. I admitted my reticence to making such a commitment but added (with a little sarcasm) that perhaps a seminary with Union's reputation could lead me in that direction, that maybe they had something to teach me. Later, another professor said matter-of-factly, "I hope you have applied elsewhere. I wouldn't want to see you put all your eggs in one basket."

All the way home, I felt hollow, empty, squished, squashed, and squelched. This had been my *dream*. Now my dream was *shattered*! When I reached my house, there was a letter from my second choice: Harvard Divinity School in Cambridge, Massachusetts. It was a letter of *acceptance*. Erasing all my feelings of rejection, this letter welcomed me warmly into the class of incoming students for the year beginning in September of 1958. I immediately replied, confirming my intention to attend.

Ironically, days later, I received another communication from Union Theological Seminary, thanking me for my visit and congratulating me upon my acceptance. Too late! I already had made my choice. I had opted for my second choice over my first choice. Maybe, somehow, *unseen*, *God* was in this, the God who is not only behind the scenes but also behind the "seens!" At Harvard Divinity School, I would encounter Jesus, experience a call to pastoral ministry, and meet the woman who would become my wife.

So it is that sometimes our dream for ourselves must be shattered in order that God's dream for us be fulfilled. That's why we resonate with the wisdom of this verse from Proverbs: "Trust in the Lord with all thine heart; and lean not unto thy own understanding. In all thy ways acknowledge him, and he shall direct thy paths" (Prov. 3:5–6, KJV).

King David had a son, and this newborn child must have arrived into his family like a dream come true. But the child got sick and was critically ill. The Bible tells us,

> David pleaded with God for the child. He fasted and went into his house and spent the nights lying on the ground. The elders of his household stood beside him to get him up from the ground, but he refused, and he would not eat any food with them. On the seventh day, the child died. David's servants were afraid to tell him that the

> child was dead, for they thought, "While the child was still living, we spoke to David but he would not listen to us. How can we tell him the child is dead? He may do something desperate." (2 Sam. 12:16–18)
>
> David noticed that his servants were whispering among themselves and he realized the child was dead. 'Is the child dead?' he asked. "Yes," they replied, "he is dead." Then David got up from the ground. After he had washed, put on lotions and changed his clothes, he went into the house of the Lord and worshiped. Then he went to his own house, and at his request they served him food, and he ate. (2 Sam. 12:19–20)
>
> His servants asked him, "Why are you acting this way? While the child was alive, you fasted and wept, but now that the child is dead, you get up and eat!" He answered, "While the child was still alive, I fasted and wept. I thought, 'Who knows? The Lord may be gracious to me and let the child live.' But now that he is dead, why should I fast? Can I bring him back again? I will go to him, but he will not return to me." (2 Sam. 12:21–23)

His personal dream was shattered. But now he was ready to awaken to *God's* larger dream for his life. What David did not know, and could not know, was that he was destined to become the ancestor of the Messiah (Matt. 1:6, 16–17).

Your dreams may get shattered; your highest hopes may be smashed. Nevertheless—unseen by us—the Lord has a way of fulfilling *his* dream for you. In a book entitled *The Rest of Your Life*, Patrick Morley wrote that the Lord, our Creator, can make use of all the ingredients of our lives, even the bad additives, to create something special, for nothing is wasted.

Morley tells the story about how years ago, at a Christian mission, a young girl tried her hand at making a cake. She put in all her ingredients but wound up with a gooey mess. She figured that her only option was to dump the whole thing out and write it off as a total loss. Edith Shaeffer happened upon the scene and, reviewing the culinary accident, was reluctant to waste all those expensive ingredients. She calculated that if she added one more ingredient, she could salvage the whole project. Out of the sticky glob, she magically created delectable noodles. And, noted the author, that's just what God can do. He is able to take the mess you've made out of your life, add his own ingredient, and transform it into something special.[1]

Therefore, place your shattered dreams—along with the shattered dreamer—into his hands. Keep on trusting the Lord, walking with the Lord, staying close to the Lord. And may all *his* dreams for you come true!

Chapter 24

SUFFERING

Personally, whenever I am confronted by my own private pain or suffering, I confess to being quick to challenge God, demanding to know, "Why have you allowed this to happen to me, your faithful servant?" In the blink of an eye, I feel disillusioned, disappointed, abandoned, deserted. All of us take suffering personally. It always seems to me that any kind of suffering—be it physical or psychological—is like a massive rock upon which our faith is either established or dashed to pieces. Most of the time we have no control over the circumstances. However, we can manage how we respond to them.

I have always treasured the words of the thirty-fourth psalm because it lets me know that even if we cannot comprehend those painful experiences we encounter in life, the Lord is still with us through it all: "I will extol the Lord at all times; his praise will always be on my lips. My soul will boast in the Lord; let the afflicted hear and rejoice. Glorify the Lord with me; let us exalt his name together." (Psalm 34:1-3 NIV)

Then the psalmist proceeds to offer his own personal testimony: "This poor man called, and the Lord heard him; he saved him out of all his troubles. The angel of the Lord encamps around those who fear him, and he delivers them. Taste and see that the Lord is good; blessed is the man who takes refuge in him." (Psalm 34:6-8 NIV)

Then the psalmist added, "The Lord is close to the brokenhearted and saves those who are crushed in spirit." (Psalm 34:18 NIV)

For all of us, there are those puzzling times in our life "when God doesn't make sense."[1] James Dobson recounted the following story about a young man named Chuck Frye, a brilliant student looking forward to a bright future. In his first year of medical school, he began to recalculate his plans. Perhaps his life's goal ought not to be the acquisition of personal wealth. Instead, he began to consider investing himself in assisting the impoverished and disadvantaged around the world.

However, by the end of a year he was feeling sick and exhausted. Eventually he was diagnosed with an insidious disease: acute leukemia. In just a few months, his promising young life was snuffed out. How could his hopeful parents see God's presence in the midst of this unmitigated tragedy? All their son had ever wanted was to do the Lord's will. It just did not make any sense to Chuck's family and friends. After all, he might have been a compassionate healer in the lives of those who were broken in both body and spirit.[2]

I once heard Dr. Tony Campolo relate the following story. A woman approached him at the end of a seminar and asked him to pray for her husband, who was struggling with cancer. Later she phoned him to say that shortly after Tony's prayer, her husband passed away. "But it's all right," she hastened to add, "because his whole attitude changed after your prayer, and we were able to enjoy the best four days of our married life." She paused, then offered this insight: "He was not cured, but he was healed." This is a subtle difference between being cured and being healed. To be cured involves our body; to be healed involves our soul.

As our Lord was hanging helplessly on the cross, stretched out between heaven and earth, dangling defenselessly before his tormentors, they taunted him. "If you are—as you say—the 'Son of God,' try coming down from that cross." They said, "He saved others, now he cannot even save himself. We will believe in you if you come down from that cross."(Matthew 27:39-42 paraphrase) He did not come down—not because he was not the Son of God, but because he was.

Long ago, the prophet Isaiah had inscribed these words: "Surely he hath borne our griefs, and carried our sorrows: yet we did esteem him stricken, smitten of God, and afflicted. But he was wounded for our transgressions, he was bruised for our iniquities: the chastisement of our peace was upon him: and with his stripes we are healed." (Isaiah 53:4-5 KJV) When I read the word *stripes*, I think of whiplashes. Through his own suffering, you and I are healed, made whole with God.

In 1 Peter comes this wonderful reassurance: the Lord is offering you "an inheritance that can never perish, spoil or fade—kept in heaven for you." (1 Peter 1:4 NIV) Beyond all the immediate material blessings we seek comes this greater blessing. Although it is not something we can see, it is nonetheless entirely real.[3] Paul wrote in Romans 8: "I consider that our present sufferings are not worth comparing with the glory that will be revealed in us. (Romans 8:18 NIV) And again in 2 Corinthians 4, "For our light and momentary troubles are achieving for us an eternal glory that far outweighs them all. So we fix our eyes not on what is seen, but on what is unseen. For what is seen is temporary, but what is unseen is eternal." (2 Corinthians 4:17-18 NIV)

In one of the churches my wife and I served, I became close friends with a young parishioner named Johnny Burke. He was in his late teens and was a very caring and empathetic person. He was also a survivor. When he was only around ten years of age, he began suffering with neurological symptoms and was eventually diagnosed with an inoperable brain tumor. It could not be excised surgically. He was given a battery of cobalt radiation treatments, but they could never be repeated. In other words, if the tumor came back, there would be no stopping it. The team of doctors did not believe that Johnny would live to be twenty.

He did, and our grateful church members gave him a huge birthday party. Though always fragile in health, Johnny had become an assistant scoutmaster, and scouts were on hand to celebrate. Shortly after his party, Johnny began to have severe headaches once again. As everyone feared, the tumor was growing relentlessly, metastasizing throughout his brain. He slowly died by inches, losing his mobility, his hearing, his eyesight.

I sat beside him, feeling broken. I desperately wanted him to stay with us in this world; he just as desperately wanted to go on to the next. He wanted to be with Jesus. Even without his eyesight, he was picturing heaven. He could see it with deeper sight.

> "No eye has seen, nor ear heard, no mind has conceived what God has prepared for those who love him."—but God has revealed it to us by his Spirit. (1 Corinthians 2:9-10 NIV. St Paul is alluding to Isaiah 64:4)

As Johnny lay dying, I understood that he was already somewhere else, somewhere beyond suffering, somewhere beyond pain, somewhere safe in the Lord's everlasting arms.

Chapter 25

HOPELESSNESS

Because we are all too human, we become so absorbed in the problems all around us—and inside us—that we're prone to be oblivious to the presence of God. We don't see him, and we're not looking for him. Instead, we try to depend upon ourselves and our own resources. One day, maybe late in the afternoon, Jesus dismissed his disciples so that he could be alone in prayer. He told them he would meet them later, and they climbed into their fishing boat (Matt. 14:22).

Soon, evening came, and darkness enveloped them. To add to their challenge, a storm arose, with strong headwinds, preventing their progress. The waves were threatening to swallow their boat (Matt. 14:24). Several of Jesus's followers were commercial fisherman, yet even they could not handle their ship. It must have plunged like a bucking bronco beneath them. And they probably imagined that they were all alone in their quandary, yet there was One who saw them clearly.

Early in the morning, Jesus came to them, and he was walking on the water. I think that means that, in some miraculous way, he transcended the storm. He was there—with them! The epiphany was so paranormal that the disciples were terrified.

> "It's a ghost!" they said, and cried out in fear. But Jesus immediately said to them: "Take courage! It is I. Don't be afraid." (Matt. 14:25–27)
>
> "Lord, if it's you," Peter replied, "tell me to come to you on the water." "Come," he said. Then Peter got down out of the boat, walked on the water and came toward Jesus. But when he saw the wind, he was afraid and, beginning to sink, cried out, "Lord, save me!" Immediately Jesus reached out his hand and caught him. "You of little faith," he said, "Why did you doubt?" (Matt. 14:28–31)

Like Simon Peter, you and I are intensely aware of the storms all around us. In the midst of our hopelessness, what we forget to look at is the face of Jesus. We look to ourselves but not to him. He is still the One who transcends all of life's storms. He is still the One who reaches out. He is still the One who saves. Long ago the psalmist wrote, "Your path led through the sea, your way through the mighty waters, though your footprints were not seen" (Ps. 77:19).

Each of us has felt hopeless at one time or another in our life. We all know what it feels like to be down in the dumps, to be in the pits. Did you ever feel that you were so far down that you could not possibly sink deeper? Did you ever believe that you didn't have a prayer? The psalmist certainly felt that way when he wrote the impassioned words of the 130th psalm:

> Out of the depths have I cried unto thee, O Lord. Lord, hear my voice: let thine ears be attentive to the voice of my supplications. If thou, Lord, shouldest mark iniquities, O Lord, who shall stand? But there is forgiveness with thee, that thou mayest be feared. I wait for the Lord, my soul doth wait, and in his word do I hope. (Ps. 130:1–5, KJV)

So we need not despair, and nothing is ever really *hopeless*. When you are in the pits, when you are at the very bottom, there is nowhere else to go but *up*. Betsie ten Boom once said that no matter how deep our despair, God's love goes even deeper.[1]

There is an instructive story related in the book of 1 Kings. It takes place during a period in Israel's history when their Hebrew faith was being compromised by idolatry. Ahab, Israel's king, was instrumental in diluting his people's faith with his religious syncretism. God's spokesman, Elijah, dared to oppose him, so a titanic struggle ensued between prophet and king. "Now Elijah…said to Ahab, 'As the Lord, the God of Israel, lives, whom I serve, there will be neither dew nor rain in the next few years except at my word'" (1 Kings 17:1). A drought lay on the land like a heavy blanket.

> After a long time…the word of the Lord came to Elijah: "Go and present yourself to Ahab, and I will send rain on the land." So Elijah went to present himself to Ahab." (1 Kings 18:1–2a)

> And Elijah said to Ahab, "Go, eat and drink, for there is the sound of a heavy rain." (1 Kings 18:41)

Now I think the prophet's message was amazing. He heard the approaching rain. There was no lightning, no thunder, no rain, no clouds, no mist, no nothing! But he *heard* the approaching rain. Here is another example of the seen and the unseen. It's also an example of the heard and the unheard. How could Elijah hear the sound of approaching rain? Because he was *listening*! That's how hope counters despair.

> So Ahab went off to eat and drink, but Elijah climbed to the top of [Mt.] Carmel, bent down to the ground and put his face between his knees. "Go and look toward the sea," he told his servant. And he went up and looked. "There is nothing

there," he said. Seven times Elijah said, "Go back." The seventh time the servant reported, "A cloud as small as a man's hand is rising from the sea."…Meanwhile, the sky grew black with clouds, the wind rose, a heavy rain came." (1 Kings 18:42–44a, 45a)

Sometimes that's how hope comes into our hearts. It starts out very small, like that little hand arising from the sea. Blink your eye and you'll miss it. But it grows until it fills the whole sky. A poet wrote,

> There shall be showers of blessing:
> This is the promise of love;
> There shall be seasons refreshing,
> sent from the Savior above.[2]

The cherished hymn "It Is Well with My Soul" was written by a heartbroken father whose crushing sorrow became a song of faith.

> When peace like a river attendeth my way,
> When sorrows like sea-billows roll;
> Whatever my lot, Thou hast taught me to say,
> "It is well, it is well with my soul."[3]

This is the story behind the writing of that great hymn. Horatio Spafford, an attorney, decided that his wife and four daughters (ages 11, 9, 7, and 2) deserved an ocean cruise to Europe. Because he needed to transact some unfinished business, he planned to join them later. His family departed with great anticipation, but something went terribly wrong.

During the early hours of November 22, 1873, while most of the sleeping passengers were oblivious to the ship's progress, it collided in the dark with another ship. In the blackness of the night, the passengers desperately struggled to escape, but in a mere twelve minutes, the cruise ship slipped beneath the surface of the sea. Gone were Horatio Spafford's four daughters, along with two hundred and twenty-two other lives. Of his family members, only his wife, Anna, had been rescued.

When the fifty-seven survivors disembarked in Cardiff, Wales, Anna sent her husband a telegram with only two words: "Saved—Alone." Distraught, he boarded another ship to take him to his wife's side and requested that when they reached the site of the tragic collision, he be informed. It was there, where his precious daughters had vanished in the waves, that he wrote his song of praise: "It Is Well with My Soul."[4]

> And, Lord, haste the day when my faith shall be *sight*,
> The clouds be rolled back as a scroll,
> The trump shall resound, and the Lord shall descend,
> Even so, it is well with my soul.[5]

No matter what joys or sorrows, what darkness or what light, "it is well" because our *hope* is in the same Lord who once said, "Take courage! It is I. Don't be afraid" (Matt. 14:27).

Chapter 26

"It Is Well with My Soul"

> O Love divine, that stooped to share
> Our sharpest pang, our bitterest tear,
> On thee we cast each earth-born care;
> We smile at pain while thou art near.[1]

I remember a story that my own pastor, Preston Haas, told me long ago. It was an incident that took place in his pastoral ministry. A man named Tom Spangler had been our Sunday school superintendent for many years and the principal of a junior high school. He was a role model, a mentor, and a man of God. Tom became a patient at Holy Redeemer Hospital, struggling against the ravages of cancer. To everyone, it was apparent that he might win some battles but eventually would lose the war.

Our pastor walked into the hospital room and asked, "How are things going for you?"

Tom answered bitterly, "Terrible! Why am I going through all of this?"

The pastor said, "I honestly don't know."

"Doesn't God know I'm suffering?"

"I'm sure he does, Tom."

"Then why doesn't he heal me? Doesn't he know what this feels like? Why doesn't he suffer too?"

There was the challenge: "Why doesn't he suffer too?"

Pastor Haas told me that he was stunned by Tom's question. He looked around the room for some answer. There on the wall of the room in this Catholic hospital was a crucifix. His eyes locked on it. "Look at that cross, Tom," he ventured. "I really don't know *why* people suffer, but I know the Lord suffers *with* us."

For many people, that's no answer at all. But for me, the cross points to the answer.

> On thee we fling our burdening woe,
> O love divine, forever dear,
> Content to suffer while we know,
> Living and dying, thou art near![2]

We have so many questions that life does not answer. I have stood beside too many hospital beds and too many caskets not to wonder. Yet above all the cacophony of mortal words is the music of God's Word:

> For I am persuaded, that neither death, nor life, nor angels, nor principalities, nor powers, nor things present, nor things to come, nor height, nor depth, nor any other creature, shall be able to separate us from the love of God, which is in Christ Jesus our Lord. (Rom. 8:38–39, KJV)

The apostle Paul described, in shorthand, his own personal experiences with affliction. In 2 Corinthians 12, he wrote, "I know a man in Christ who fourteen years ago was caught up to the third heaven. Whether it was in the body or out of the body I do not know—God knows… He heard inexpressible things, things that man is not permitted to tell" (2 Cor. 12:2, 4b). We cannot know just what Paul saw and experienced, but it was definitely out of this world.

Now comes the letdown for Paul: "To keep me from becoming conceited because of these surpassingly great revelations, there was given me a thorn in my flesh, a messenger from Satan, to torment me" (2 Cor. 12:7). Some biblical scholars speculate that the "thorn in the flesh" might have been malaria, a very prevalent disease in the regions in which Paul traveled.

> Three times I pleaded with the Lord to take it away from me. But he said to me, "My grace is sufficient for you, for my power is made perfect in weakness." Therefore I will boast all the more gladly about my weaknesses—For when I am weak, then I am strong." (2 Cor. 12:8–9a, 10b)

Sometimes the afflicted are marvelously healed; sometimes they aren't. But always our prayer must be that God might be glorified either in healing or in death. As Jesus faced his own death, he prayed, "Father, glorify your name" (John 12:28a). In Romans we read, "I consider that our present sufferings are not worth comparing with the glory that will be revealed in us" (Rom. 8:18). Again, in 2 Corinthians, it says, "For our light and momentary troubles are achieving for us an eternal glory that far outweighs them all" (2 Cor. 4:17).

One woman told the story of her journey into darkness and then into spiritual light. Throughout her childhood, she had struggled with failing eyesight. By the time she reached ninth grade, her eyeglasses no longer compensated for her dimming vision. The lights were going out for her. The doctors at an eye institute in Miami reached a diagnosis: *retinitis pigmentosa*. That meant her retinas would continue to deteriorate until she would see nothing at all. She and her parents were shocked by the grim prognosis, by the inevitability of blindness.

Upon arriving home, this young girl walked directly to her piano, sat down, and began to play a hymn. Up to that moment, she never had played by ear. Having had lessons for a few years, she always played the piano by reading the notes. Now, however, she began to play without having any music to read. She began playing "It Is Well with My Soul."

Later, she said that the real miracle that day was not her piano improvisation but the genuine sincerity she experienced within her heart. For the Lord had made it well with her soul. Since that day she has come to realize that nothing may be well with our circumstances but everything may be well with our souls because of his presence within our hearts.[3]

> When peace like a river attendeth my way,
> When sorrows like sea-billows roll;
> Whatever my lot,
> Thou hast taught me to say,
> "It is well, it is well with my soul."[4]

Chapter 27

LISTENING PRAYER

Whenever any of us goes to a restaurant, we typically pay for our meal and then include a tip. The waitstaff counts on those tips. Do you know the original meaning of that term? "To ensure prompt service." We want—and even demand—prompt and efficient service, believing that we are entitled to it. My best friend once sagely remarked that most church attenders probably are "tipping" God. It is their way of encouraging supernatural promptness and service.

In his book *In Defense of the Faith*, Dave Hunt suggested that a whole lot of so-called religious people use prayer as their preferred method of choice for encouraging the Lord to fulfill their personal agenda.[1] I remember hearing about a frustrated young woman who said in her prayer, "Dear Lord, I don't want to be selfish. I am asking nothing for myself. But please send my parents a wonderful son-in-law."

The focus of our spiritual life ought to be prayer, but if you are at all like me, you spend more time talking *at* God than listening *to* him. Prayer listens as well as speaks. We are not to be instructing him about our own agenda; we are to be listening for his. That is what it means to call him Lord. We call Jesus our Lord and Savior, yet those two terms are not synonymous. Most want Jesus to be their Savior;

not many want him to be their Lord, for then they would have to listen to him.

I am sharing with you an episode from my own life where I was obliged to listen in my prayer. During a convocation of pastors, another minister solemnly approached me and, with a sense of urgency, said, "Jerry, please accompany me to my room and join me in prayer. There's something special I believe we need to be praying for." On one hand I was relieved to be exiting the meeting with its boring dry-as-dust speeches. On the other hand, I was not exactly thrilled to be escaping into a prayer meeting. It might be a case of going out of the frying pan into the fire. It might be more boring than the convocation. Nevertheless, I dutifully abandoned my seat and followed my ministerial colleague.

"Well," I asked him candidly, "what is it that you and I are supposed to be praying about?"

"I cannot tell you," he answered.

"Then how can I know? How can I pray with you?"

He said emphatically, "You will just have to listen to the Lord."

I was stunned by his nonanswer. I mean, up till now I thought that prayer was all about talking to God, not listening to him. Aware of my confusion, my friend Jon added, gently, this explanation: "Jerry, there's a fellow pastor here that is in need. I feel that the Lord wants to do something special for him. I personally believe I know what it is we are to do, but I am waiting to see if the Lord tells you. I really need confirmation. I am waiting to see if he gives you the same answer he has given me."

So I was supposed to stop chattering and to start listening. This was difficult for someone who tends to fill up all the silences with senseless verbiage. I waited and waited, sensing that the lack of direction was attributable not to God but to me. I did not hear anything except the sounds of my own digestive tract. Not a big thunderous voice. Not a tiny pip-squeak voice. Not a shout or a whisper. Nothing. I kept imagining what a big disappointment I would be to my confident friend were I to come up empty-handed.

Empty-handed! Suddenly I became aware of my hands. My hands, always ice-cold, were gradually growing warm and then hot.

THE SEEN AND THE UNSEEN

My perpetually cold, clammy hands were almost on fire. As I listened to the Lord, I began to realize that we were supposed to lay hands on our fellow pastor and pray for him to be healed. When I shared this knowledge with Jon, he was ecstatic. "Yes, that's it. Thank you, Jesus." And that night we laid hands on him and prayed. He, and we, were bathed in the warmth of God's presence, power, and love.

"So, we fix our eyes not on what is seen, but on what is unseen. For what is seen is temporary, but what is unseen is eternal." (2 Corinthians 4:18 NIV) Behind the scenes, behind the "seens," there is more than meets the eye. In the beautiful forty-sixth psalm the poet writes, "God is our refuge and strength, a very present help in trouble.—Be still, and know that I am God." (Psalm 46:10a KJV) Listen with faith; watch with faith. "One sees clearly only with the heart; what is essential is invisible to the eye."[2]

A certain missionary named Everett Howard was reflecting on his long career and recounting how it all began. One fateful night, as a young man, he crept into a chapel where he could sit alone and undisturbed. It would just be he and God. He brought with him tablet paper and a pen so that he might write down all the promises he was intending to make to the Lord. He wrote, for instance, that he would faithfully read his Bible, tithe his money, utilize his talents, etc. Then he studied his long list of promises and took some pride in the thought that he was serious and sincere.

Satisfied that the list was comprehensive and that he had included everything, he signed his name on the bottom of the page and lovingly laid it on the altar. Alone, all by himself, he anxiously awaited the Lord's response. He thoroughly expected God to do something—give some supernatural sign of divine approval. Perhaps there would be a flash of flame or at least a small wisp of smoke. Nothing. Well, maybe he had overlooked something on his rather extensive list.

He picked it up and looked at it again, but everything seemed to be in order. He laid it back upon the altar. Then he heard the Lord speaking to his heart. The Lord was telling him to pick up the paper and crumple it up. Then take another piece of blank paper. Leave it completely blank. The Lord was saying through the silence, "Just sign your name on the bottom and let me fill in the rest."

This missionary added that over his thirty-six years in the mission field, he had felt blessed, guided, and directed. There were times of great suffering and deprivation, times of deep joy and fulfillment.[3] He was glad that the Lord did the infilling and the filling in. What each of us needs to do is listen.

Chapter 28

The Twenty-Third Psalm

Perhaps the most beautiful psalm ever written is the incomparable twenty-third psalm. It begins with a reverberating affirmation of faith:

> The Lord is my shepherd; I shall not want.
> (Ps. 23:1, KJV)

That statement is more than theological gibberish; it defines the most crucial relationship you can have: you and God! Notice the psalmist doesn't abstractly say, "The Lord is *a* shepherd" or even "The Lord is *the* shepherd." He says, "The Lord is *my* shepherd." And because he's *my* shepherd, "I shall not want!" Just as the sheep know in their bones that the shepherd will take care of *them*, so too can you know that the shepherd will take care of *you*. Jesus said, "I am the good shepherd; I know my sheep and my sheep know me (John 10:14)...My sheep listen to my voice; I know them, and they follow me. I give them eternal life, and they shall never perish; no one can snatch them out of my hand" (John 10:27–28).

> He maketh me to lie down in green pastures.
> (Ps. 23:2a)

That means we can trust him to lead us to where he already has made provision for us. There we can rest assured. "For thus saith the Lord God, the Holy One of Israel; In returning and rest shall ye be saved; in quietness and in confidence shall be your strength" (Isa. 30:15a, KJV).

> He leadeth me beside the still waters. (Ps. 23:2b)

Still waters! Every sheep wears a heavy woolen overcoat and knows instinctively that it could drown. Therefore sheep won't drink from moving water. Sometimes the shepherd will dam a stream to make a quiet pool so that his sheep may drink without fear.[1] In much the same way, the Good Shepherd wants to allay *your* fears. "God has said, 'Never will I leave you; never will I forsake you.' So we may say with confidence, 'The Lord is my helper; I will not be afraid'" (Heb. 13:5b–6a).

> He restoreth my soul. (Ps. 23:3a)

Sheep need reassurance. There's a moment every day when each sheep will approach the shepherd just to be nuzzled, whispered to, and stroked. Then the comforted sheep returns to the fold.[2] Even so, the Lord cares about *you*. When you are coming apart, you need to come apart with *him*. Whenever you feel spiritually or mentally exhausted, whenever you feel like giving up, you need to come to him in prayer. He stoops down, picks you up, dusts you off, and sets you on your feet again. He "restores your soul."

> He leadeth me in the paths of righteousness for
> his name's sake. (Ps. 23:3b)

Not for the "name," the reputation we have made for ourselves, but for the Name he has made for himself! Not because of how good *we* are but because of how good *he* is! The prophet Isaiah wrote his beautiful prophecy: "He shall feed his flock like a shepherd: he shall gather the lambs with his arm, and carry them in his bosom, and shall gently lead those that are with young" (Isa. 40:11, KJV). It is clearly an uplifting experience to be *led* by him. Again, there's that favorite hymn that says,

> He leadeth me: O blessed thought!
> O words with heavenly comfort fraught!
> Whate'er I do, where'er I be,
> Still 'tis God's hand that leadeth me.
>
> ...Lord, I would place my hand in thine,
> Nor ever murmur nor repine;
> Content, whatever lot I see,
> Since 'tis my God that leadeth me.[3]

A man named Alexander Maclaren became aware of the power of the insight below while he was just a young man.

> Yea, though I walk through the valley of the shadow of death, I will fear no evil: for thou art with me. (Ps. 23:4a)

He had been offered his first job in Glasgow, Scotland. This job was only six miles away from his home but was separated from it by a deep, cavernous ravine. There were those who thought this ravine was haunted and were afraid to traverse it in broad daylight, let alone at night. Maclaren would be gone at his job all week and then return home for the weekend.

His father, who never had been without him before, instructed him to come home the very night his work was over. Young Alexander's heart froze. He thought about his having to negotiate that ravine in the dark. So he casually informed his father that he'd just as soon wait to leave until the next morning. At which point his father informed Alexander that he would return home that last night of work!

Overruled, Alexander lived all week in fear of his walk home. When the fateful evening arrived, he lugged his suitcase to the edge of the ravine and stood there, staring into the pitch black, paralyzed.

Then he heard footsteps and a familiar voice, "Son, I've come to walk you home." Together they walked home through the valley.[4]

> Thy rod and thy staff they comfort me.
> (Ps. 23:4b, KJV)

The sheep has no natural weapons with which to defend itself. It easily could fall victim to any predator. But the shepherd carries a two- or three-foot-long club, a rod, to protect the sheep against its enemies. And a staff, which is close to eight feet in length, with its end upturned, making the familiar "shepherd's crook!" If the sheep were to stumble and slip down into a gully, the shepherd could extend his staff, hook it around the narrow chest of the helpless animal, and pull it back to safety.[5] Furthermore, a little nudge with the staff will guide the sheep the way the shepherd wants it to go.[6] In the same way, he nudges and guides *you*.

> Thou preparest a table before me in the presence of mine enemies. (Ps. 23:5a, KJV)

Poisonous plants proved fatal to sheep that nibbled them. The caring shepherd would dig them up, pile them up, and burn them up, transforming the floor of the wilderness into a table.[7] In the midst of all those booby traps that might rob us of our joy, or even our lives, there appears the Lord's Table: the Eucharist. And like those sheep, we give thanks.[8]

> Thou anointest my head with oil; my cup runneth over. (Ps. 23:5b, KJV)

The good shepherd positioned himself at the entrance to the sheepfold and examined each sheep as it entered. Sometimes it happened that one had been cut or wounded or scraped in some way, and the shepherd would then anoint it with olive oil and let it drink deeply.[9] Once Jesus said, "If anyone is thirsty, let him come to me and drink" (John 7:37b).

THE SEEN AND THE UNSEEN

> Surely goodness and mercy shall follow me all the
> days of my life: and I will dwell in the house of
> the Lord for ever. (Ps. 23:6, KJV)

That rock-strong faith enabled my friend Urban Jones to say—as he faced death—"If my faith as a Christian is true, then I can't lose. If I live, the Lord is with me. And if I die, I'll be with the Lord. But I can never be separated from His love." I later realized that his words were a paraphrase of Romans 8, where Paul wrote, "For I am persuaded, that neither death, nor life, nor angels, nor principalities, nor powers, nor things present, nor things to come, nor height, nor depth, nor any other creature, shall be able to separate us from the love of God, which is in Christ Jesus our Lord" (Rom. 8:38–39, KJV).

The seen and the unseen! Like the young man, Alexander Maclaren, we see ahead of us only the inky blackness, not the Light! We see only the scary ravine, not the Father's presence! Like the sheep, we see only our own vulnerability, not the rod and the staff of the shepherd! We see only the wilderness, not the table that he has prepared! We see only death, not eternal life!

> So we fix our eyes not on what is seen, but on
> what is unseen. For what is seen is temporary, but
> what is unseen is eternal. (2 Cor. 4:18)

Once upon a time, there was a contest held at a state fair to determine who could best recite the beautiful twenty-third psalm. There were only two contestants, and they could not have been more different from one another. The first was a young man, elegant in dress and eloquent in speech, who had been thoroughly educated in elocution and drama. The second was an old farmer, clothed in his work-a-day overalls.

The young man was first to approach the stage, and he was every inch an orator. When he finished, the audience rose to their feet and erupted in applause. Then it was the turn of his only challenger: the old farmer. He lumbered to his feet and, in a broken voice, began not to say but to pray the psalm. When he finished, he was greeted by silence.

Once again the young actor rose to his feet and moved to center stage. He addressed the crowd, explaining what just had transpired. "When I spoke, you accorded me a standing ovation. When this old man spoke, you sat in hushed silence. That's because I know the *psalm*, but he knows the *Shepherd*."[10]

Chapter 29

"The Silence of God"[1]

Far back in Israel's history, writing at the beginning of the sixth century BC, a prophet anticipated an impending geopolitical disaster. In response to his vision, Habakkuk wrote these ringing words of affirmation: "Though the fig tree does not bud and there are no grapes on the vines, though the olive crop fails and the fields produce no food, though there are no sheep in the pen and no cattle in the stalls, yet I will rejoice in the Lord, I will be joyful in God my Savior" (Hab. 3:17–18).

In spite of the apparent hopelessness of his circumstances, the prophet would continue to fix his eyes on the Lord. In spite of the troubles that surrounded and threatened to engulf him, Habakkuk would focus on God's presence.

> So we fix our eyes not on what is seen, but on
> what is unseen. For what is seen is temporary, but
> what is unseen is eternal." (2 Cor. 4:18)

In one church I pastored in Philadelphia, a teenage girl came to the breakfast table one morning and informed her mother that she had a sore throat.

"How long have you had it?" the mother inquired casually.

"Two weeks," her daughter answered.

"Two weeks!" asked the mother with alarm. "Why didn't you tell me this before? Why did you wait so long?"

Her daughter, Lynn, replied sarcastically, "Oh yeah! I probably have leukemia, and I'm going to die."

Unknown to both mother and daughter in that moment, Lynn had called it. She had unwittingly pronounced both her diagnosis and prognosis. The fifteen-year-old's life span suddenly was abridged.

Ruth, Lynn's mother, later recalled, "When Lynn said those words, a cold chill went right through me. I immediately made an appointment with our doctor, who initially diagnosed her as having mononucleosis. But when the tests proved negative, he had to revise his diagnosis. 'Ruth, it's not good news. I sincerely wish that Lynn had mono. Your daughter has leukemia!' I was stunned. I remembered vividly Lynn's offhanded remark at the breakfast table: 'I probably have leukemia, and I'm going to die.'"

Suffice it to say, our whole church community fervently prayed for Lynn to be healed. We held an all-night prayer vigil with half-hour shifts. We stormed the gates of heaven with our prayers and petitions, but the heavens turned to brass, and our prayers came bouncing back. God was *silent*.

I became a platelet donor for my young parishioner, but this was just a stop-gap protocol. Her condition continued to deteriorate, unabated by the best medical techniques and technologies. She died. And here's the tragic irony! The very day that I would be taking my own daughter on a trip to Israel, I presided over the funeral of Lynn Batezel. Here was one daddy burying his little girl while in a few short hours, this other daddy would be escorting his own daughter to the Holy Land. I gazed at Lynn in her casket, holding her beloved stuffed teddy bear in her lifeless arms, and wept. All I could hear around me was *the silence of God*. It was deafening.

There's a troublesome episode that's recounted in the fifteenth chapter of Matthew, related in a handful of words: "Jesus withdrew to the region of Tyre and Sidon. A Canaanite woman from that vicinity came to him, crying out, 'Lord, Son of David, have mercy on me! My daughter is suffering terribly from demon possession.' Jesus did not answer a word" (Matt. 5:21–23a). He didn't answer. We struggle with *the silence of God!* In his book by that same title, Helmut Thielicke said that this silence is the greatest challenge to our faith.[2]

Jesus did not answer the woman; Jesus remained strangely silent, yet he heard her. The fact that he was silent did not mean he was deaf.[3] I always have believed that there is a matter of timing and that the Lord will answer in *his* time, not ours. Isn't that the hardest time to believe in him? We interpret his silence as indifference. The psalmist, amid the maelstrom of his feelings, wrote, "To you I call, O Lord, my Rock; do not turn a deaf ear to me. For if you remain *silent*, I will be like those who have gone down to the pit" (Ps. 28:1; emphasis mine)

The disciples did not want the woman there in the first place, whimpering and whining and wailing for Jesus to help. They "came to him and urged him, 'Send her away, for she keeps crying out after us'" (Matt. 5:23b). First of all, from their perspective, this woman was a Gentile, a non-Jew, and Gentiles just took up space. They were a waste of oxygen. God should not waste any time or energy on these godless creatures. Secondly, she was a hysterical woman! She kept pestering them, intruding upon the serenity of their morning. "Just get rid of her!" they said, "Dump her!"

Then Jesus spoke to the woman directly. "'I was sent only to the lost sheep of Israel.' The woman came and knelt before him. 'Lord, help me!' she said" (Matt. 15:24–25). She hung in there. She didn't stop praying. Had she no pride? In all my fifty years of ministry, I've never seen pride help anybody. This wasn't the time for pride; it was the time for humility. "He replied, 'It is not right to take the children's bread and toss it to their dogs'" (Matt. 15:26). That sure sounds like rejection to me. Doesn't it sound that way to you? Doesn't it sound like Jesus was closing the door on her? Slamming the door in her face? It sounds unmistakably like that to me. End of interview! Case closed!

Then quick as a flash, she answered, "'Yes, Lord, but even the dogs eat the crumbs that fall from their master's table'" (Matt. 15:27). She wasn't looking for the main course, just the crumbs, the leftovers! We, like that Gentile mother, come to the Lord, recognizing that he is our last, best hope. The blind poet Fanny Crosby wrote a hymn that is the prayer of each of us:

> Pass me not, O gentle Savior—
> Hear my humble cry!
> While on others Thou art calling,
> Do not pass me by.[4]

"Then Jesus answered, 'Woman, you have great faith! Your request is granted.' And her daughter was healed from that very hour" (Matt. 15:28). Had Jesus simply been playing games with her? Was this some sort of mental gymnastics? I don't think so. I believe that he was testing her motivation—even as he is apt to test yours. I once heard an evangelist give an altar call at the conclusion of his message. He was calling on each listener to make a decision for his or her life and for his or her eternity. Then he added this caveat: "Jesus is inviting you to come to him. But don't come unless you really mean business with God!" This Gentile woman came forward fearlessly and shamelessly because she really meant business with the Lord.

There is so much in life we don't see. We do manage to see all the problems that confront us, the dilemmas that entrap us, and the diseases that assault us. However, we don't manage to see the grace of the Lord Jesus Christ, who once said, "I am the bread of life: he that cometh to me shall never hunger; and he that believeth on me shall never thirst…and him that cometh to me I will in no wise cast out" (John 6:35, 37b, KJV).

In his book *The Silence of God*, Helmut Thielicke offered this illustration: You can walk around the *outside* of a cathedral, observing its slate-gray windows. Then you can return home and honestly declare that you have seen the cathedral's unremarkable slabs of stained glass. Yet it's not exactly true. You saw only the *outside*. It's not until you are *inside* the sanctuary that you can observe the radiant beauty of the illuminated stained glass windows.[5] So it is that the only way we'll be able to *see* what is ordinarily *unseen* is to stand on the *inside* of faith and to recognize the all-embracing love of God.

Chapter 30

"AT EVERY CORNER"

The Concluding Message

In Leslie Weatherhead's insightful book *Prescription for Anxiety*, there is a chapter entitled "Help at Every Corner." In it, the author tells the story of a man named Hugh Redwood, who had come to a critical crossroads in his life, just as each of us will do periodically. He came to a standstill, paralyzed by indecision. He was mentally and emotionally incapacitated, unable to process all the data, sort it out, or think it through. At just this moment, a dear friend invited him to stay at his home, to come there for a little R and R.

In the course of that first evening, they sat together, engaging in superficial conversation. His host couldn't help noticing his guest's obvious discomfiture. Hugh Redwood had a faraway look; his heart and mind were somewhere else. So his friend gently asked, "Would you like to take some time for yourself and escape this chatter? I've already prepared your room upstairs." And he had. It was a palatial room that instantly made its guest feel welcome. It had a cozy fire burning in the fireplace, a lounge chair positioned in front of it, and a nightstand beside it.

On that nightstand was an open Bible. Hugh glanced at it and saw a verse highlighted: Psalm 59:10a, which read, "The God of my mercy shall prevent me" (KJV). Now that phrase doesn't make much sense to an English reader living centuries after that translation was made. During the intervening years, language has changed. Today the word *prevent* is used to mean "hinder" or "impede." But in 1611 it meant "precede," "go before." So in context, the verse doesn't mean that God will *stop* us, but rather that he'll *lead* us. And in the margin of the Bible on the nightstand someone had sensitively inscribed this paraphrase: "My God, in His loving kindness, *shall meet me at every corner.*"

Suddenly the significance of that verse made an impact on Hugh's mind, and the Holy Spirit stirred his heart. Hugh Redwood later said that the truth of that Scripture verse bathed his dark soul in brilliant light. He could walk forward with new confidence and assurance.[1]

Just as Hugh discovered, we, too, have a God who, in his loving kindness, will meet us at every corner of our lives. In your life, I'm certain that there have been those magical moments when someone seemed to go ahead of you, opening all the right doors and perhaps closing the wrong doors. You possibly never even noticed but just nonchalantly sauntered along, strolling through every open door with never a thought that someone had *prepared* the way, someone unseen, for there's always more than meets the eye! Sometimes I imagine that when we arrive in heaven, we'll discover that our entire journey was programmed by a loving Father who yet, paradoxically, offered us the freedom to make our own choices. We walk through the right door because he meets us at every corner. We see that he *prepares* the way. The psalmist said, "He leadeth me in the paths of righteousness for his name's sake" (Ps. 23:3b, KJV).

One the first Palm Sunday, as Jesus and his disciples were climbing up the far side of the Mount of Olives, he sent two followers on ahead with instructions:

> "Go to the village ahead of you, and as you enter it, you will find a colt tied there, which no one has ever ridden. Untie it and bring it here. If

> anyone asks you, 'Why are you untying it?' tell him, 'The Lord needs it.'"
> Those who were sent ahead went and found it just as he had told them. As they were untying the colt, its owners asked them, "Why are you untying the colt?"
> They replied, "The Lord needs it."
> They brought it to Jesus, threw their cloaks on the colt and put Jesus on it. (Luke 19:29b–35)

Reading between the lines, we can speculate that the donkey's owners were part of Jesus's wider circle of support, that they, too, were his followers. And the phrase "The Lord needs it" was most likely a prearranged signal. The point is that Jesus already had *prepared* for his Palm Sunday entrance into Jerusalem. He would enter the city mounted upon a humble beast of burden.

> Rejoice greatly, O daughter of Zion! Shout, Daughter of Jerusalem! See, your king comes to you, righteous and having salvation, gentle and riding on a donkey. (Zech. 9:9a)

Days later would come the celebration of the Passover, and Jesus would say to Peter and John,

> "Go and make preparations for us to eat the Passover."
> "Where do you want us to prepare for it?" they asked.
> He replied, "As you enter the city, a man carrying a jar of water will meet you. Follow him to the house that he enters, and say to the owner of the house, 'The Teacher asks: Where is the guest room, where I may eat the Passover with my disciples?' He will show you a large upper room, all furnished. Make preparations there." (Luke 22:8b–12)

So once again, a series of prearranged signals! They were supposed to follow a man carrying a water jar. But men did not carry water jars; that was *women's* work. It would be tantamount to saying, "Look for the man carrying a lady's pocketbook!"[2] Furthermore, the disciples were to use a specific phrase, "The Teacher asks, Where is the guest room?" The point again is that Jesus already had *prepared* for the Last Supper. It's written in the twenty-third psalm, "Thou *preparest* a table before me in the presence of mine enemies" (Ps. 23:5a, KJV; emphasis mine).

Then on that fateful night, Jesus said,

> Let not your heart be troubled: ye believe in God, believe also in me. In my Father's house are many mansions: if it were not so, I would have told you. I go to *prepare* a place for you. And if I go and *prepare* a place for you, I will come again, and receive you unto myself; that where I am there ye may be also. (John 14:1–3 KJV; emphasis mine)

The God who met you at the first corner of your life will meet you at the last.

Once Jesus had said, "No one takes [my life] from me, but I lay it down of my own accord" (John 10:18a). I believe this was literally true. Apparently, no crucified victim just hung limply suspended on the cross. Instead, in order to exhale, he was obliged to raise his body on the cross. Then he'd drop back down in exhaustion. It became a rhythmic movement, which could last for hours or even days. At last, to finish off the dying man, one of the soldiers would break his legs. Unable then to lift himself up, he slowly would strangle to death.

When Jesus cried out, "Father into thy hands I commend my spirit" (Luke 23:46a, KJV), I believe that he literally allowed his body to slump down on the cross. He gave himself over to death. That's why his legs did not have to be broken; he already was dead. It's written in Scripture, "These things happened so that the scripture would be fulfilled [Exodus 12:46b]: 'Not one of his bones will be broken'"

(John 19:36). So it was that Jesus literally *laid down* his life for us. He planned for it; he *prepared* for it.

When Jesus let himself down on the cross, he let down everybody. After the crucifixion, distraught and humiliated, his disciples went back to doing the only thing they knew how to do: fish! All night long, they fished. They netted nothing. Just like all those years they had wasted following Jesus of Nazareth! Rack it up to another "net" loss!

Then as the delicate pastels of the dawn streaked across the slate-gray sky, they spotted a stranger standing on the beach. He told them where to cast their nets. Responding to his authoritative tone, they hauled in their catch. And with a sense of recognition, they perceived who he was—and is. "It is the Lord" (John 21:1–7)!

> When they landed, they saw a fire of burning coals there with fish on it, and some bread. Jesus said to them, "Bring some of the fish you have just caught… Come and have breakfast." None of the disciples dared ask him, "Who are you?" They knew it was the Lord. (John 21:9–10, 12)

Jesus had *prepared* breakfast for them. Their covenant with the Host was restored. In his gracious forgiveness, he had "cast all their sins into the depths of the sea" (Mic. 7:19b, KJV)

Quoting Isaiah, the apostle Paul wrote, "No eye has seen, no ear has heard, no mind has conceived what God has *prepared* for those who love him" (1 Cor. 2:9, quoting Isa. 64:4; emphasis mine). So be on tiptoe with anticipation, for he will meet you at every corner of your life. Amen.

A Closing Prayer

Holy God, Creator of space and time,
Yet timeless in eternity,
Breathing your Spirit into all that is,
Standing both without and within,
We've come in quietness
That we might hear you.

Holy God, Redeemer of the lost,
Graciously stepping into our lives,
Saying, "Look for me, I am here,"
We come in faith
That your warmth, your light, your love
Will make us come alive again.

In those thin places
Where heaven touches earth,
Where eternity touches time,
Like gears which mesh at every point,
Where minutes stop and moments start,
Please make us come alive again.

Speak deeply to our soul,
Deep calling unto deep.
Open our eyes to your presence,
Open our ears to your music,
That we might become channels of your grace
Into the life of another. Amen.

—J. Crossley

ENDNOTES

Notes to the Foreword
1. Robert McAfee Brown, *The Bible Speaks to You* (Louisville, Kentucky: The Westminster Press, 1955), 53.

Notes to Chapter 1
1. C. Bernard Ruffin, *Padre Pio: The True Story*, revised and expanded (Huntingdon, Indiana: Our Sunday Visitor Publishing Division, 1991), 143.
2. Walter B. Knight, *Knight's Master Book of New Illustrations*, "Can You Feel The Tug?" by Chester E. Shuler (Grand Rapids, Michigan: Wm. B. Eerdmans Publishing Company, 1956), 189.
3. Michael Green, *The Empty Cross of Jesus* (Downers Grove, Illinois: InterVarsity Press, 1984), 43.

Notes to Chapter 2
1. Reginald Heber (1783–1826), Hymn "Holy, Holy, Holy;" verse 3 (written 1826).
2. Timothy Keller, *The Reason for God: Belief in an Age of Skepticism* (New York, NY: Penguin Group Inc., 2008), 122–123.

3. Fanny J. Crosby (1820–1915), Hymn "He Hideth My Soul;" verse 1 and chorus (written 1890).
4. Walter Chalmers Smith (1824–1908), Hymn "Immortal, Invisible;" verse 1a (written 1867).
5. Brennan Manning, *The Ragmuffin Gospel: Embracing the Unconditional Love of God* (Sisters, Oregon: Multnomah Books, 1990), 119–120; Story originally told by Walter J. Burghardt, *Tell The Next Generation* (New York: Paulist Press, 1980), 43.

Notes to Chapter 3
1. Reverend Martin Wiznat, pastor of St. Paul's Lutheran Church in the Olney neighborhood of Philadelphia (5th Street and Nedro Avenue), 1958.
2. Elizabeth Elliott, *In The Shadow Of The Almighty* (Peabody, MA: Hendrickson Publishers, 1958), 15 and 108 (quoting her husband Jim Elliott's Journal, entry October 28, 1949).

Notes to Chapter 4
1. Elizabeth Sherrill, *Daily Guideposts 2006* (Carmel, NY: Guideposts, 2006), meditation for May 1, 2006; "The Smallest Seeds Our Daily Bread," 124.
2. Based on an illustration from John R. W. Stott, *Understanding The Bible* (Minneapolis, Minnesota: WorldWide Publications, published as a Special Crusade Edition for the Billy Graham Evangelistic Association, 1972), 160–161.
3. Joseph H. Gilmore (1834–1918), Hymn "He Leadeth Me," verse 1 (written 1862).

Notes to Chapter 5
1. (Source unknown to me.)
2. Suggested by Michael P. Green, editor, *Illustrations For Biblical Preaching (*Grand Rapids, Michigan: Baker Book House, 1982, 1985, 1989), 421, illustration # 1538.

3. Michael P. Green; *op. cit.*; 389, illustration # 1439.

Notes to Chapter 6
1. Matthew Arnold (1822–1888), Stanzas from the Grande Chartreuse, stanza 15.
2. John Greenleaf Whittier (1807–1892), Hymn "I Know Not What The Future Hath," vss. 1 and 5.
3. John Henry Newman (1801–1890), Hymn "Lead, Kindly Light," v. 1.
4. Roy L. Smith, *Tales I Have Told Twice* (Nashville, Tennessee: Abingdon Press, 1964), p. 15; quoted by Gaston Foote, *How God Helps* (Nashville, Tennessee: Abingdon Press, 1966), 35.

Notes to Chapter 7
1. Paul Rader, Hymn "Only Believe" (text: Mark 9:23).
2. Maxie Dunnam, *Perceptions: Observations on Everyday Life* (Wilmore, Kentucky: Bristol Books, 1990), 34.
3. Charles L. Allen, *Perfect Peace* (Minneapolis, Minnesota: Grason, 1979), 104–105.

Notes to Chapter 8
1. Elisha A. Hoffman, Hymn "Leaning on the Everlasting Arms," verse 3 (written 1887).
2. Catherine Jackson, *The Christian's Secret of a Happy Life for Today: A paraphrase of Hannah Whitall Smith's Classic)* (published for the Billy Graham Evangelistic Association by World Wide Publications, 1303 Hennepin Avenue, Minneapolis, Minnesota, @1979 by Catherine Jackson), 31–32.
3. Leith Anderson, *When God Says No* (Minneapolis, Minnesota: Bethany House Publishers, 1996 by Leith Anderson), 205–206.
4. Philip Doddridge (1702–1751) Hymn "How Gentle God's Commands," verses 1 and 4.
5. Catherine Jackson, op. cit., pp. 33–34.

6. Ibid., 35.
7. John Greenleaf Whittier (1807–1892), Hymn "Immortal Love-Forever Full," verses 2a, 4 (written 1866).
8. "Jimmy" Kitchen, Pocono Lake, PA, 1961.

Notes to Chapter 9
1. *Leadership* (Carol Stream, IL: Leadership, Spring Quarter 1992), 49; article entitled "Finishing Well: by Wes Thompson; Cheyenne Wells, Colorado.
2. Charles R. Page II, *Jesus & The Land* (Nashville, Tennessee: Abingdon Press, 1995), 52.
3. *Ibid.* 177, footnote 18, paragraph 2.

Notes to Chapter 10
1. Edgar T. Chrisemer, *Every Common Bush* (Boston, MA: Bruce Humphries, Inc., Publishers, 1953), 161.

Notes to Chapter 11
1. The title of this chapter is the title of a book by Philip Yancey, *Disappointment With God: Three questions no one asks aloud* (Grand Rapids, MI: Zondervan Publishing House, 1988).
2. John Greenleaf Whittier (1807–1892), Hymn "I Know Not What The Future Hath," vss. 1 and 5.
3. Somewhere around 1990 at Evangelical United Methodist Church in New Holland, PA.

Notes to Chapter 12
1. Marva J. Dawn, *Reaching Out Without Dumbing Down: A Theology of Worship for the Turn-of-the-Century Culture* (Grand Rapids, MI: Wm. B. Eerdmans Publishing Company, 1995), 92–93.
2. Clarence Edward Macartney, *Macartney's Illustrations: Illustrations from the Sermons of Clarence Edward Macartney* (Whitmore & Stone, 1945 & NY and Nashville: Abingdon Press, 1946), 118a.

3. Charles Wesley, Hymn "Jesus, Lover of My Soul," verse 1 (written 1740).
4. Dr. James Dobson, *When God Doesn't Make Sense* (Wheaton, Illinois: Tyndale House Publishers, Inc., 1993), 113.
5. *Ibid.* 114.

Notes to Chapter 13
1. William Cowper (1731–1800), Hymn "There Is a Fountain Filled with Blood," vss. 1a and 2a (written 1772).
2. *Ibid.* verse 2b.
3. Charlotte Elliott (1789–1871), Hymn "Just As I Am," vss. 1–2 (written 1835).

Notes to Chapter 14
1. Fanny J. Crosby, Hymn "All The Way My Savior Leads Me," vss. 1a & 2a (emphasis mine) (written 1875).
2. Maxie Dunnam, *Perceptions: Observations on Everyday Life* (Wilmore, Kentucky: Bristol Books, 1990), "The Salvation Army," 39.
3. John Sutherland Bonnell, *Psychology For Pastor and People*, rev. ed. (New York: Harper & Brothers, Publishers, 1948), 86–87.
4. *Ibid.*, 87–89.
5. Fanny J. Crosby, Hymn "All The Way My Savior Leads Me," vs. 2a (written 1875).

Notes to Chapter 15
1. Roy L. Smith, *From Saul to Paul: The Making of an Apostle* (Nashville, Tennessee: Tidings, 1962 by Tidings), 43.
2. Ibid., 44.
3. Corrie ten Boom with Jamie Buckingham, *Tramp for the Lord* (Carmel, New York: Guideposts, 1974 by Corrie ten Boom & Jamie Buckingham), 65–66.
4. Ibid., 67–68.

Notes to Chapter 16
1. Catherine Marshall, *Light In My Darkest Night* (Old Tappan, NJ: Chosen Books–Fleming H. Revell Company, 1989), 66–67.
2. Walter B. Knight, *Knight's Treasury of Illustrations* (Grand Rapids, Michigan: Wm. B. Eerdmans Publishing Company, 1963), "As God Sees It," 447–448.

Notes to Chapter 17
1. John Greenleaf Whittier (1807–1892), Hymn "Dear Lord and Father of Mankind," vs. 2 (1872).
2. *Guideposts* (Carmel, NY: Guideposts Associates, Inc., vol. 41, No. 2, Apr. 1986), "One Simple Word From God," Marion Bond West, 10–11.
3. *Ibid.* 12.
4. *Ibid.* 12–13.

Notes to Chapter 18
1. Dr. Grant Martin, *Transformed By Thorns* (Wheaton, Illinois: Victor Books, A Division of SP Publications, Inc., 1985), 21.
2. Dan Weaver, *His Weavings,* vol. 2 (Duncanville, Texas, 1998), 16.
3. Billy Graham, *Hope for The Troubled Heart* (Dallas, Texas: Word Publishing, 1991), 144.
4. *Ibid.* 94 (using an illustration by Rev. Calvin Thielman).

Notes to Chapter 19
1. William D. Longstaff, Hymn "Take Time to Be Holy," (based on 1 Peter 1:16), vss. 1a and 2a (written 1882).

Notes to Chapter 20
1. William Barclay, *The Gospel of John,* vol. 1 (chapters 1 to 7) rev. ed., The Daily Study Bible Series (Philadelphia, PA: The Westminster Press, 1975), 97.
2. *Ibid.*, 101.

3. Michael P. Green, *Illustrations for Biblical Preaching* (Grand Rapids, Michigan: Baker Book House, 1982), Illustration # 1295, "Sorrow," 349–350.

Notes to Chapter 22
1. Keith Miller, *Habitation of Dragons* (Waco, Texas: Word Books, Publishers, 1970), 183–184.
2. Francis of Assisi (1181–1226), "The Prayer of St. Francis."

Notes to Chapter 23
1. Patrick M. Morley, *The Rest Of Your Life* (Nashville, Tennessee: Thomas Nelson, Publishers, Inc., 1992), 148.

Notes to Chapter 24
1. Dr. James Dobson, *When God Doesn't Make Sense* (Wheaton, Illinois: Tyndale House Publishers, Inc., 1993 by Tyndale House Publishers, Inc).
2. Ibid., 3–4.
3. Stacy and Paula Rinehart, *Living in the Light of Eternity* (Colorado Springs, Colorado: NAVPRESS, a ministry of the Navigators, 1986 by Stacy & Paula Rinehart) 145.

Notes to Chapter 25
1. Corrie ten Boom, with John and Elizabeth Sherrill (Old Tappan, NJ: Spire Books – Fleming H. Revell Company, 1971), 217.
2. Daniel W. Whittle, Hymn "There Shall Be Showers of Blessing" (based on Ezekiel 34:26), vs. 1 (written 1883).
3. Horatio G. Spafford, Hymn "It Is Well with My Soul," vs. 1 (written 1873).
4. *Power for Living* (brochure) (Colorado Springs, Colorado: SP Publications, vol. 55, Number 3, June-July-August, 1997), "It Is Well with My Soul," story by Patricia Thompson, 3–5.
5. Horatio G. Spafford, Hymn "It Is Well with My Soul," vs. 4 (written 1873).

Notes to Chapter 26
1. Oliver W. Holmes (1809–1894) Hymn "O Love Divine That Stooped to Share," vs. 1.
2. Ibid., vs. 4.
3. *Decision Magazine* (Charlotte, NC: Billy Graham Evangelistic Association; editors-in-chief: Billy Graham, Franklin Graham; vol. 48, Number 5, May 2007), "Faith Through Darkness" by Jennifer Rothschild, 31–32.
4. Horatio G. Spafford, Hymn "It Is Well with My Soul," vs. 1 (written 1873).

Notes to Chapter 27
1. Dave Hunt, *In Defense of the Faith* (Eugene, Oregon: Harvest House Publishers, 1966 by Dave Hunt), 27–28.
2. Antoine de Saint-Exupéry, *The Little Prince* (1900–1944), 21.
3. Dr. James Dobson, *Emotions*: Can you Trust Them? (Minneapolis, Minnesota: Worldwide Publications, 1980 by Regal Books, A Division of G/L Publications; Ventura, California) 135–138.

Notes to Chapter 28
1. From a brochure based on a book by Charles L. Allen, *God's Psychiatry* (Grand Rapids, Michigan: Fleming H. Revell Company, 1953).
2. *Ibid.*
3. Joseph H. Gilmore (1834–1918) Hymn "He Leadeth Me," vss. 1 and 3 (written 1862).
4. Walter B. Knight, *Knight's Treasury of Illustrations* (Grand Rapids, Michigan: Wm. B. Eerdmans Publishing Company, 1963), "Father's Presence" from D. C. Roy Angell (in *Iron Shoes*), 294.
5. Allen; *op. cit.*
6. Phillip Keller, *A Shepherd Looks at Psalm 23* (Grand Rapids, Michigan: Zondervan Publishing House, 1970; 10th printing August 1972), 100–101.

7. Allen; *op. cit.*
8. Keller; *op. cit.* 111–112.
9. Allen; *op. cit.*
10. Charles L. Allen, *God's Psychiatry* (Carmel, NY: Guideposts Associates, Inc.), 26–27 (First published in Old Tappan, NJ: Fleming H. Revell Company, 1953).

Notes to Chapter 29
1. The title of this chapter is the title of a book by Helmut Thielicke, *The Silence of God* (Grand Rapids, Michigan: Wm. B. Eerdmans Publishing Company, 1962).
2. *Ibid.*, 12.
3. Charles Caldwell Ryrie, *The Miracles of Our Lord* (Nashville, Tennessee: Thomas Nelson, Publishers, 1984), 117.
4. Fanny J. Crosby (1820–1915), Hymn "Pass Me Not, O Gentle Savior," vs. 1 (written 1868).
5. Thielicke; *op. cit.* 92.

Notes to Chapter 30
1. Leslie D. Weatherhead, *Prescription for Anxiety* (New York & Nashville: Abingdon Press, 1956), 113.
2. Ben Witherington, *New Testament History: A Narrative Account* (Grand Rapids, Michigan: Baker Academic, A Division of Baker Book House Company, and Pater Noster Press, Carlisle, Cumbria, UK, 2001), 141 (with its attendant footnote 10).

CPSIA information can be obtained
at www.ICGtesting.com
Printed in the USA
FSHW021142150320
68049FS